EYEWITNESS
PLANETS

Written by
Carole Stott

Pluto, a dwarf planet

Saturn V rocket blasts off the launchpad

Penguin Random House

REVISED EDITION

DK DELHI
Senior Art Editor Vikas Chauhan
Editor Ankita Gupta
Art Editor Aparajita Sen
Senior Managing Editor Rohan Sinha
Managing Art Editor Govind Mittal
DTP Designers Harish Aggarwal, Pawan Kumar, Rajdeep Singh
Jackets Designer Juhi Sheth
Senior Jackets Coordinator Priyanka Sharma-Saddi

DK LONDON
Senior Editor Carron Brown
Art Editor Chrissy Checketts
US Editor Jennette ElNaggar
US Executive Editor Lori Cates Hand
Managing Editor Francesca Baines
Managing Art Editor Philip Letsu
Senior Production Editor Andy Hilliard
Senior Production Controller Poppy David
Senior Jackets Designer Surabhi Wadhwa-Gandhi
Jacket Design Development Manager Sophia MTT
Publisher Andrew Macintyre
Associate Publishing Director Liz Wheeler
Art Director Karen Self
Publishing Director Jonathan Metcalf

Consultant Giles Sparrow

FIRST EDITION
Consultant Dr. Jacqueline Mitton

DK LONDON
Senior Editors Camilla Hallinan, Jenny Sich
Senior Designer Spencer Holbrook

DK DELHI
Senior Art Editor Sudakshina Basu
Editor Priyanka Kharbanda
Picture Researcher Sumedha Chopra
Picture Research Assistant Esha Banerjee
Managing Jackets Editor Saloni Singh
Picture Research Manager Taiyaba Khatoon
Managing Editor Kingshuk Ghoshal
Managing Art Editor Govind Mittal

This American Edition, 2023
First American Edition, 2017
Published in the United States by DK Publishing
1745 Broadway, 20th Floor, New York, NY 10019

Copyright © 2017, 2023 Dorling Kindersley Limited
DK, a Division of Penguin Random House LLC
24 25 26 27 10 9 8 7 6 5 4 3 2
009–335449–Apr/2023

All rights reserved.
Without limiting the rights under the copyright reserved above, no part of this publication may be reproduced, stored in or introduced into a retrieval system, or transmitted, in any form, or by any means (electronic, mechanical, photocopying, recording, or otherwise), without the prior written permission of the copyright owner.
Published in Great Britain by Dorling Kindersley Limited

A catalog record for this book is available
from the Library of Congress.
ISBN 978-0-7440-7993-7 (Paperback)
ISBN 978-0-7440-7994-4 (ALB)

DK books are available at special discounts when purchased in bulk for sales promotions, premiums, fund-raising, or educational use. For details, contact:
DK Publishing Special Markets,
1745 Broadway, New York, NY 10019
SpecialSales@dk.com

Printed and bound in China

For the curious
www.dk.com

This book was made with Forest Stewardship Council™ certified paper—one small step in DK's commitment to a sustainable future. For more information go to www.dk.com/our-green-pledge

Earth's Pacific Ocean

Earth-orbiting satellite

Close-up, false-color view of Saturn's north pole

Jupiter outweighs all seven other planets combined

EYEWITNESS
PLANETS

Parker Solar Probe

A meteorite fragment in false color

A young rocky planet bombarded by rocks from space

Jupiter's Great Red Spot, captured by the infrared James Webb Space Telescope

Ingenuity Helicopter

NASA's Perseverance rover

Contents

Phoenix lander

6 Planet Earth and its neighbors
8 What is a planet?
10 Changing worlds
12 Skywatching
14 Space age exploration
16 The sun
18 Mercury
20 Venus
22 Earth
24 Water world
26 Living planet
28 The moon
30 Exploring the moon
32 Mars
34 The Red Planet
36 Roving on Mars
38 Asteroids
40 Jupiter
42 Jupiter's moons
44 Saturn
46 Saturn's rings
48 Saturn's moons
50 Visiting the giants
52 The outer solar system
54 Uranus
56 Neptune
58 The outer dwarfs
60 Comets
62 Exoplanets
64 Did you know?
66 Solar system facts
68 Timeline
70 Glossary
72 Index

Planet Earth and its **neighbors**

Part of the family of space objects called the solar system, Earth and seven more planets formed about 4.6 billion years ago. They each orbit the sun, as do billions of smaller bodies such as asteroids, and others far beyond the planets.

Planetary solar system

The sun is our local star. Its gravity holds the solar system together. Following elliptical orbits—stretched, circular paths—around the sun, the eight planets and the asteroids together orbit in a disc-like plane that extends about 2.8 billion miles (4.5 billion km) out from the sun.

Inner planets

The four planets closest to the sun are also the solar system's smallest. Often called the inner or rocky planets, all four are balls of rock and metal, but with very different surfaces. Earth has life and oceans; Mars is a frozen desert; Venus has a volcanic surface; and Mercury is covered with craters.

Mercury | Venus | Earth | Mars

Inner planets

> **The sun** contains more than **99.8%** of all **the mass** in the **Solar System.**

Outer giants

Known as the giants, Jupiter, Saturn, Uranus, and Neptune are the outermost and largest of the solar system planets. They are also the most massive, being made of the most abundant material—hydrogen. Each has a thick atmosphere, rather than a solid surface, and a ring system.

Jupiter | Saturn | Uranus | Neptune

Outer giants

6

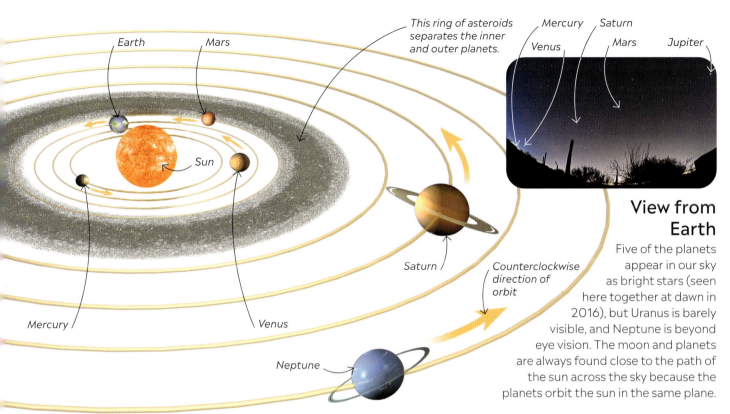

View from Earth

Five of the planets appear in our sky as bright stars (seen here together at dawn in 2016), but Uranus is barely visible, and Neptune is beyond eye vision. The moon and planets are always found close to the path of the sun across the sky because the planets orbit the sun in the same plane.

Planetary moons

There are at least 219 moons in the solar system. Earth has one, and Mars has two; Mercury and Venus have none. All four giants have large families of moons—Jupiter and Saturn have at least 80 each, including Saturn's Tethys and Titan (right).

Birth of the solar system

The solar system formed from a spinning cloud of gas, dust, and ice particles. As gravity pulled material inward, the central region became denser and hotter, forming our star about 4.6 billion years ago. Unused material settled into a disc around the sun (above) and formed the planets.

Orbit and spin

Most planets orbit in a roughly flat plane around the sun. Planets closer to it complete their orbits quicker than the rest. Each one also spins on an axis line between its poles. In most cases, this axis is tilted, giving rise to changing seasons.

STRUCTURE

Beyond Neptune is the Kuiper Belt of rock and ice bodies, including the dwarf planets Pluto and Eris. More distant still is Sedna, at more than 900 times the Earth–sun distance. Surrounding all of this is the Oort Cloud, home of comets, which marks the limit of the sun's influence.

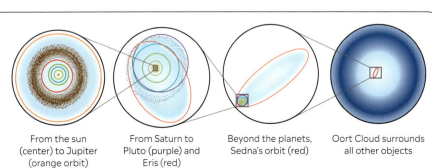

From the sun (center) to Jupiter (orange orbit) | From Saturn to Pluto (purple) and Eris (red) | Beyond the planets, Sedna's orbit (red) | Oort Cloud surrounds all other objects

7

What is a planet?

For centuries, people have labeled Earth and other huge, round bodies orbiting the sun as planets. Recent discoveries have led to a formal definition, and two new classes—dwarf planets and exoplanets. Just as Earth and seven more planets orbit the sun, exoplanets orbit other stars. There may be tens of billions of exoplanets orbiting stars in the Milky Way Galaxy.

The planet Mercury—false color highlights different rock types

Defining a planet

The word "planet," from the Ancient Greek for "wanderer," was used to describe so-called wandering stars—planets moving across the starry sky. In 2006, the International Astronomical Union (IAU) defined a planet as a body orbiting the sun that is massive enough for its gravity to make it nearly round, and which has cleared other objects out of its path.

Dwarf planet

Discovered in 1930, Pluto was classed as a planet. But then Eris, a body more distant and seemingly larger than Pluto, was found in 2005. Both are far smaller than the other planets and follow elongated orbits among other objects. In 2006, the IAU introduced the class of dwarf planet. A dwarf planet orbits the sun and is massive enough for its gravity to make it round but has not cleared the neighborhood around its orbit.

Pluto with its moon Charon (upper left)

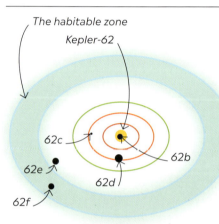

Kepler-62 System

THE HABITABLE ZONE

Earth is in the sun's habitable zone, a region where liquid water can exist and allow life to form and flourish. Any closer to the sun, Earth would be so hot that its water would evaporate away. Any farther, Earth would be so cold, its water would freeze. Exoplanets in habitable zones could harbor life. Two planets, 62e and 62f, orbit the star Kepler-62 within its habitable zone.

The orange sun-like star HD 189733 has one known exoplanet.

Planet HD 189733b—a gas giant larger than Jupiter—orbits its star in 2.2 days.

Exoplanet

Exoplanets are small compared to their stars, which also outshine them—making them doubly difficult to detect. We know of more than 5,000 exoplanets. Most of those known orbit stars relatively close to the sun, but a few far more distant exoplanets have been discovered, including some floating alone in space.

The solar system is in an arm of the Milky Way Galaxy.

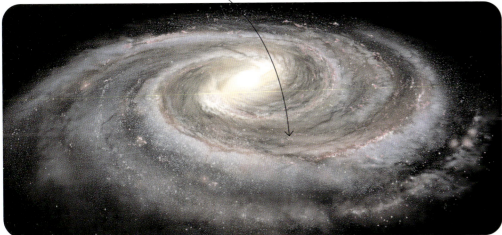

The world of astronomy

While planetary astronomers look at planets in our solar system and beyond, in recent decades other experts have begun to look at the prospects for life on more distant planets. There are even projects underway to search for radio signals and other signs of alien life.

Our place in the universe

The sun and its planets lie within the Milky Way Galaxy, a vast system of stars, gas, and dust that has at least 200 billion stars. More than 2,600 of those close to us have exoplanets. Astronomers think at least one in every 20 stars has exoplanets orbiting it. And there could be as many stars with exoplanets in the universe's other 200 billion or more galaxies.

Naming the planets

The planets were named in ancient times after Greek or Roman gods, and we still use their Greek or Roman names today. For instance, Venus is named after the Roman goddess of love (left). Of the two planets discovered in modern times, Uranus is named after the Greek god of the sky, and Neptune after the Roman god of the sea.

Giant dishes like this one in West Virginia may one day detect alien radio signals.

9

Changing worlds

Early in their history, the planets were bombarded by rocks from space that scarred the surfaces of the rocky inner planets. Over millions of years, volcanic activity, land movement, and the action of water, wind, and atmosphere have continued to shape the landscapes and features of the planets.

Mars's Santa Maria Crater is about the size of a football field

Cratering
Millions of impact craters scar the rocky planets and their moons. They form when rocks from space smash into the surface and gouge out material. The largest craters are hundreds of miles across. The rate of impact has slowed since the most intense period of bombardment, 3.5 billion years ago.

Rocky balls
The rocky planets took shape as material left over from the sun's formation clumped together into four hot, molten balls. As they cooled, they settled into layers, creating a rocky surface and metal core. More rocks from space crashed into the young planets, forming craters. Inside the planets, heat from radioactivity made the rock molten and some of it flowed out in volcanic eruptions.

1995   2009
2014   2017

Giant planets
As the young giant planets shrank, their cores grew hotter and their upper atmospheres formed bands where storm clouds rage. In the last few years, Jupiter's long-lived Great Red Spot (left) has been shrinking by at least 124 miles (200 km) each year.

Tungurahua volcano, Ecuador

Volcanism
Heat from inside the rocky planets and some moons has powered different kinds of volcanoes. Over time, volcanic activity (volcanism) has tended to reduce as these bodies have cooled down. Earth is still volcanic, but its crust is thickening and volcanism will eventually stop.

Hot Venus, cool Earth

Young Venus and Earth both had a thick atmosphere of carbon dioxide and water. Closer to the sun, Venus's water was broken up by the sun's energy, leaving a thick carbon-dioxide atmosphere (above). On cooler Earth, the atmosphere thinned as water fell as rain and carbon dioxide gas combined into rocks that locked it in. Much later, plants released oxygen into the air.

Surface building

The surfaces of the rocky planets are shaped by large-scale movements in their crusts over millions of years. As the young planets cooled and shrank, their surfaces cracked. Mercury's cliff Carnegie Rupes formed in this way. A false-color image shows it at the edge of the higher ground (red) cutting across cratered terrain (blue).

Erosion

Landscapes change through erosion—the wearing away of surface material by water and wind. On Earth, ocean waves change shorelines, rivers carve valleys, and glaciers pull underlying rock with them. Wind picks up material and deposits it at new sites. It also wears away rock surfaces, slowly sculpting new shapes (right).

Low land in Mars's northern hemisphere may have held an ocean of water.

Liquid water

As young Earth cooled, atmospheric steam condensed, water fell, and oceans formed. Young Mars also had liquid water in lakes and seas, but the planet has since cooled. Some water escaped via its upper atmosphere and the rest became frozen.

Skywatching

Humans have always watched the sky. The first people to study it made patterns from the stars and identified five planets. They observed the sun, moon, and planets moving against the background sky. The introduction of the telescope four centuries ago revealed many more space objects. Today, we know that the solar system is a tiny part of one galaxy in a vast universe of galaxies.

Heart of the universe
Earth was long thought to be at the center of the universe, orbited by the sun, moon, and planets (above). In 1543, Polish scholar Nicolaus Copernicus realized that the sun is at the center and that the planets, including Earth, all orbit the sun.

First observations
Ancient peoples used the sun's movement, and the changing shape of the moon, to keep track of time. Around 4,000 years ago, the Babylonians drew the first constellations—imaginary patterns around stars—and recorded the movements of the planets. At the same time, ancient Britons were completing Stonehenge (right). Its stones align with the rising or setting sun at certain times of year.

Sliding tube used for focusing

Using the telescope
Early telescopes—such as the one built by Italian astronomer Galileo Galilei—had lenses and were as powerful as a pair of simple binoculars today. From 1609, Galileo saw mountains on the moon, four moons of Jupiter, and Venus's phases. Modern-day telescopes use mirrors to collect the light from distant objects. The bigger the mirror, the more we see.

Surface features
As telescopes improved, they revealed details on planets' surfaces. In the 1870s, Italy's Giovanni Schiaparelli drew maps (above) of Mars's dark, linear features, which he called *canali* (channels). Others then mistook them for canals built by a Martian civilization—in fact, they are an optical illusion.

Expanding universe

Until the 18th century, the solar system was thought to end at Saturn. This changed with the discoveries of Uranus, Neptune, and the first worlds in the Kuiper Belt. We now know of many planetary systems in the Milky Way Galaxy, itself just one of many galaxies (below).

Sizing up the solar system

In 1609, German mathematician Johannes Kepler showed that planets orbit in an ellipse (an elongated circle), and those near the sun orbit faster than those farther away. Years later, astronomers worked out the masses of the planets (amount of material they are made of). Jupiter's mass is almost 2.5 times that of the other seven combined.

 EYEWITNESS

Henrietta Leavitt
In 1912, US astronomer Leavitt (1868–1921) made a crucial discovery without even looking at the sky. When comparing photographs of a star over time, she realized that the star's brightness could be used to calculate its distance from Earth. This later helped calculate the size of the universe.

Observatories

Several telescopes—each protected within its own building—together make an observatory. At their mountaintop locations, the air is dark, still, dry, and thin, giving the clearest possible view into the universe. The laser beam shown left shoots out of a telescope at the Paranal Observatory in the Atacama Desert, Chile.

Space age exploration

Buzz Aldrin on the moon, photographed by Neil Armstrong

Robotic spacecraft have been exploring the solar system since 1959. Far from home, in conditions no human could endure, they have investigated the planets, a host of moons, two dwarf planets, asteroids, comets, and the sun. Mostly about the size of a family car, they carry scientific instruments that test conditions on other worlds and transmit their findings home, making far distant worlds familiar.

Early exploration

The first missions to another world were the Luna craft sent by the Soviet Union to the moon. Luna 1 was the first to leave Earth's gravity, in 1959. Luna 9 was the first to soft land on the moon, in 1966. Lunokhod 1 (left) was the first rover to explore the moon. It landed in 1970 and roved across 6.5 miles (10.5 km) of its surface.

Lunokhod's cameras guided the driver on Earth who steered it around.

Mariner missions

Between 1962 and 1973, US Mariner missions made the first flybys of Venus, Mars, and Mercury. Mariner 9 (right) was the first craft to orbit another planet, arriving at Mars in 1971. The final mission, Mariner 10, was the first to visit two planets, Venus and Mercury.

Mariner 9 started returning images of Mars in January 1972.

👁 EYEWITNESS

Mae Jemison
US astronaut Mae Jemison (b.1956) broke barriers as the first Black female astronaut when she flew NASA's space shuttle *Endeavour* in 1992. She was one of the agency's first "mission specialists"—astronauts trained to carry out scientific experiments in space.

More than 33 robotic probes have now explored beyond Earth's orbit.

Sending astronauts to the moon

Twelve American men have walked on the surface of the moon, arriving two at a time on Apollo landing craft. The first, Apollo 11's Eagle, touched down on July 20, 1969. Just over six hours later, on July 21, Neil Armstrong became the first man to step onto the lunar surface, followed by Buzz Aldrin. Their trip to the moon and back was 953,054 miles (1.5 million km).

The Apollo 11 spacecraft was carried inside the upper part of the rocket.

Lower sections contained fuel and engines. These detached and fell away as the rocket climbed higher and reached Earth orbit.

A Saturn V rocket blasted off from Cape Canaveral, on July 16, 1969, launching Apollo 11 on its trip to the moon.

Cameras provided views of Mars's north polar region.

Artist's impression of Phoenix landing in 2008

Landing craft

Spacecraft use parachutes and small rockets to control their descent and make a soft (controlled) landing. The first soft landing on a planet was made by Venera 7 on Venus in 1970, but it survived for just under an hour in the corrosive atmosphere. Mars is more hospitable—four craft have successfully landed and worked there for longer periods.

Bristling with equipment

Each spacecraft carries a dozen or so scientific instruments, including several cameras, as seen here on the Curiosity rover on Mars. In this selfie taken by another camera, the large round eye is ChemCam, which includes a laser and telescopic camera. Below are two rectangular-shaped cameras, and at either side of them, a pair of navigation cameras.

Perseverance rover

NASA's Perseverance rover touched down on Mars in 2021, on a mission to search for past life and habitable environments. The six-wheeled rover is equipped with an array of cameras, drills to collect rock samples, and instruments to analyze the minerals it finds.

Each wheel has its own motor.

In-depth orbits

Spacecraft have orbited six of the solar system planets, from Mercury out to Saturn. By circling these worlds, they can make systematic studies of them. Whole planets can be mapped—and changes recorded—on a daily, monthly, or yearly basis. Juno (right) arrived at Jupiter in 2016 and moved into a polar orbit to start its scientific mission.

Three solar panels around Juno's hexagonal body provide electrical power.

The sun

Our local star generates vast amounts of energy, which is released into space and fuels life on Earth. Spacecraft monitor activity—from sunspots to huge jets of gas—and help forecast its effect on Earth. In the future, the sun will dramatically expand in size, destroying Earth.

Huge solar eruptions

Our local star

The largest and most massive body in the solar system, the sun accounts for more than 99 percent of the system's mass. It is a ball of hot gas—mostly hydrogen and helium—with no solid surface. In its core, nuclear fusion converts hydrogen to helium, producing energy that is most familiar to us as heat and light.

The sun's influence on life

The sun warms Earth and powers the water cycle (see p.24). Through photosynthesis, plants convert sunlight into chemical energy, as carbohydrates. These nourish animals that eat the plants. Photosynthesis also releases oxygen, which is vital to life.

Studying the sun

The sun is best studied from space, and a number of satellites continuously monitor it from a safe distance. The Parker Solar Probe (launched in 2018) has a daring orbit that takes it within 6 million miles (10 million km) of the sun's surface to measure conditions in its searing hot atmosphere.

The body of the probe can withstand temperatures of up to 2,511°F (1,377°C).

Solar wind

The sun constantly emits a stream of tiny particles called the solar wind, which shapes the magnetic field around planets and causes auroras. These spectacular light displays (above) occur when solar wind particles are drawn into the atmosphere above Earth's poles, collide with atoms, and cause them to give off light.

Sunspots

Dark, temporary patches on the sun's surface called sunspots are cooler regions where the sun's magnetic field interrupts rising heat. The number of spots varies in an 11-year cycle that also affects other forms of solar activity. The cycle's next peak, or solar maximum, is expected to be in 2025, and its next solar minimum will probably be around 2030.

A large sunspot seen in October 2014 could fit 10 Earths across it.

Coronal mass ejections

Made of billions of tons of gas, a coronal mass ejection speeds away from the sun (above). If it travels in Earth's direction, it can cause a solar storm. Solar storms can damage satellites, disrupt communications, cause surges in power lines, and trigger an aurora.

👁 EYEWITNESS

Cecilia Payne-Gaposchkin
In 1925, British-born American astronomer Cecilia Payne (1900–1979) analyzed light from the sun and other stars, discovering what they are made of—mostly the gases hydrogen and helium. In 1956, she became the first female professor at Harvard University.

Solar eclipse

The sun's atmosphere extends far beyond its visible surface. Normally invisible, the outermost corona can be seen when the sun is eclipsed (below). A total solar eclipse occurs when the moon is directly between the sun and Earth, covering the sun's face.

In the future

In about 5 billion years, the sun will run low on hydrogen and expand, engulfing Mercury, Venus, and Earth. Before then, its intense heat will kill all life, evaporate oceans (above), and turn Earth molten.

Mercury

Sun-baked Mercury is the solar system's innermost planet. It has a huge iron core and a rocky, barren surface covered in craters. The sun shines seven times brighter than on Earth, but Mercury's atmosphere is far too thin to retain the heat, so it is freezing cold at night.

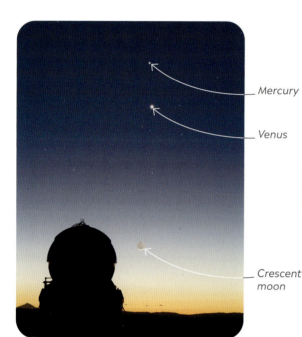

Mercury

Venus

Crescent moon

View from Earth
Mercury is never far from the sun in our sky and is usually hidden by the sun's light. But six times a year—during spring and fall—we see Mercury well, when its orbit brings it into view first on one side of the sun and then the other for about two weeks at a time.

Fast mover
Named after the swift-footed messenger of the Roman gods, Mercury speeds around the sun faster than any other planet. It takes just 88 days to complete one orbit. Yet Mercury spins on its axis very slowly, rotating once in just under 59 days, and completes just three spins in two orbits. The combination of slow spin and fast orbit means there are 176 days between one sunrise and the next.

The Amaral Crater was named after Brazilian artist Tarsila do Amaral.

Rocky surface
Mercury's rocky surface has hardly changed over the past 3 billion years. The impact craters found all over the planet formed when asteroids smashed into young Mercury. Its smooth plains formed when volcanic lava flowed over parts of its surface. Long ridges and cliffs are the result of Mercury's surface crust shrinking unevenly as the young planet cooled.

The Caloris Basin is one of the largest craters in the solar system.

Magnetometer measures Mercury's magnetism

Sunshade protects Messenger's instruments

Tolstoj, a large and ancient impact crater, is named after Russian writer Leo Tolstoy.

Bashō Crater is 47 miles (75 km) wide and is named after Japanese poet Matsuo Bashō.

Mercury is covered in craters—named after artists, writers, and musicians—because there has been no large-scale renewal of its surface since it was young.

Messenger investigates

Only two spacecraft have been to Mercury. In 1974–1975, Mariner 10 made three flybys, imaging almost half of the planet. Launched in 2004 (left), Messenger flew by Mercury three times before moving into orbit around the planet in 2011. By the end of its mission in 2015, it had mapped all of Mercury.

Mosaic imaging

Messenger's two cameras imaged Mercury's surface bit by bit. Each area imaged is 300 miles (500 km) wide. Once fitted together, the overlapping images gave a detailed view of the entire planet.

Caloris Basin

Mercury's impact craters range from small, bowl-shaped ones to the huge Caloris Basin, which is 960 miles (1,550 km) wide. In this false-color image by Messenger, dull orange highlights volcanic lava that flooded the basin floor. Craters that have exposed the original floor are blue. Younger craters are white.

BepiColombo

Launched in 2018, the multi-part BepiColombo probe is due to enter orbit around Mercury in 2025. Its European orbiter will study the planet's surface and interior, and a smaller Japanese one will study its magnetosphere, the region dominated by the planet's magnetism.

Venus

Almost as big as Earth, Venus orbits about twice as far from the sun as Mercury, but its surface temperature of 867°F (464°C) makes it the hottest planet of all. Its suffocating atmosphere hides a landscape of lava plains and volcanoes.

Atmosphere
Venus's carbon-dioxide atmosphere extends about 50 miles (80 km) above the surface. Its layers of cloud contain sulfuric acid droplets. Venus takes eight months to rotate, but the high clouds speed around Venus in just four days.

Venus has the thickest and densest atmosphere of all the rocky planets.

LOOKING THROUGH THE CLOUDS

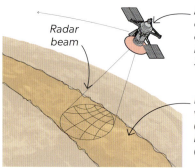

Radar beam

Magellan completed each circuit of Venus in less than 3.5 hours.

Each strip imaged was 10,600 miles (17,000 km) long and 12 miles (20 km) wide.

Orbiting Venus in 1990–1994, NASA's spacecraft Magellan used radar pulses to peer through the clouds. The signals that bounced back from the surface built up images in strips, which once combined, gave us our current global view.

Dali Chasma is a system of canyons and troughs more than 1,240 miles (2,000 km) long.

First surface view
The Venera craft were the first to land on Venus's surface. Venera 9 sent back a black-and-white view in 1975. In 1982, Venera 13 took the first color images (left).

Woman's world

This radar view by Magellan shows Venus's rocky surface, with huge volcanoes, lava plains, canyons, and impact craters formed in the last 500 million years, after the main era of volcanism. Venus is named after the Roman goddess of love. All but one of its surface features have women's names.

Shield volcanoes are built from a succession of eruptions of runny lava.

A pancake dome forms when thick lava erupts slowly.

An arachnoid volcano has fracture lines radiating out from its center.

Maat Mons is named after an Egyptian goddess.

Volcanic surface

More than 85 percent of Venus is covered in volcanic lava. Hundreds of the volcanoes that released the lava are shield volcanoes, with gentle slopes built up by successive lava flows. The smaller arachnoid volcanoes, named for their spider-web-like appearance, and the flat-topped pancake domes are unique to Venus. Most of the volcanoes are thought to be extinct.

Maat Mons

Magellan data has been used to create this computer-generated image of the shield volcano Maat Mons (right). It is the tallest volcano on Venus, rising 5 miles (8 km) above the surrounding landscape. Lava flows extend for hundreds of miles across the plains in the foreground.

Named after Queen Isabella I of Castille, Isabella crater is 108 miles (175 km) across.

Greenhouse effect

Most of the sunlight reaching Venus is reflected back into space by the top layer of its clouds, making the planet bright and easy to see from Earth. A small amount of sunlight gets through the clouds, warming the rocky surface. Heat released from the rock adds to the warming process. The clouds work like the glass in a greenhouse, keeping heat in.

About 80 percent of sunlight is reflected off Venus's clouds.

The thick layers of cloud stop heat from Venus escaping into space.

About 20 percent of the sunlight reaches Venus's surface.

Radiation from the sun-warmed ground is absorbed by carbon dioxide in Venus's atmosphere and cannot escape into space.

Earth

Our home planet is unique for its liquid water oceans and the presence of life. The largest of the four inner planets, Earth is made of rock and metal and gets denser and hotter toward its core. Surrounding it is a nitrogen-rich atmosphere protecting life below.

Earth in space
In 2018, an environmental satellite GOES-17 captured this view of Earth, showing wispy white clouds, deep blue oceans, and pale brown continents of land that cover more than a quarter of Earth's surface.

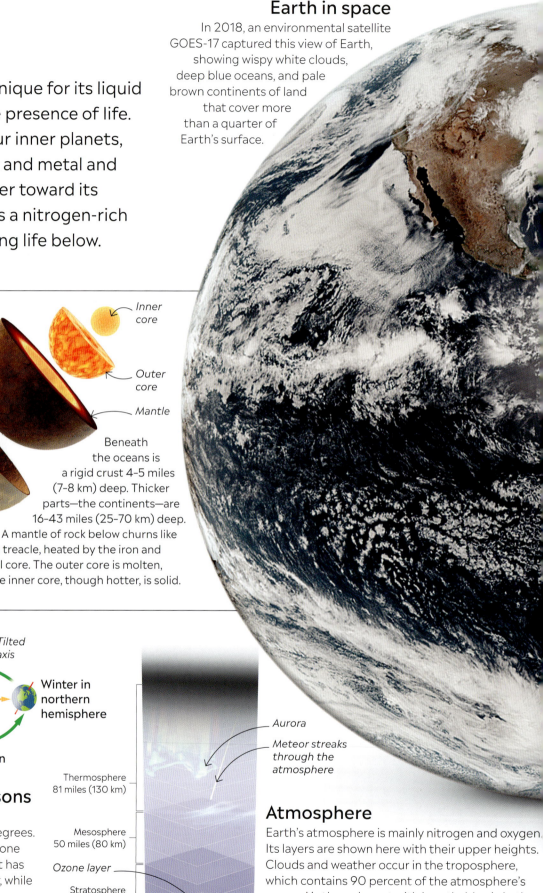

INSIDE EARTH

Oceans, Crust, Inner core, Outer core, Mantle

Beneath the oceans is a rigid crust 4-5 miles (7-8 km) deep. Thicker parts—the continents—are 16-43 miles (25-70 km) deep. A mantle of rock below churns like thick treacle, heated by the iron and nickel core. The outer core is molten, but the inner core, though hotter, is solid.

Orbit, spin, and seasons

Northern spring, Tilted axis, Winter in northern hemisphere, Northern summer, Equator, Northern fall

Earth's spin axis is not upright, but tilted at an angle of 23.4 degrees. This causes the seasons. When one hemisphere points to the sun, it has the warm, long days of summer, while the other hemisphere points away and experiences winter. Six months later, the seasons reverse.

Thermosphere 81 miles (130 km)
Mesosphere 50 miles (80 km)
Ozone layer
Stratosphere 31 miles (50 km)
Troposphere 6 miles (10 km)

Aurora, Meteor streaks through the atmosphere

Atmosphere

Earth's atmosphere is mainly nitrogen and oxygen. Its layers are shown here with their upper heights. Clouds and weather occur in the troposphere, which contains 90 percent of the atmosphere's gas and is the only part with breathable air. In the stratosphere, the ozone layer absorbs harmful radiation from the sun. Beyond this, the atmosphere thins until it merges with space.

Tectonic plates

Earth's crust is joined to the top of the mantle, in the lithosphere. This is split into tectonic plates – seven large ones (left) and many smaller ones. Lying on top of the semi-molten mantle, the plates move at about the same speed that fingernails grow.

Eurasian plate
North American plate
Pacific plate
South American plate
Antarctic plate
African plate
Australian plate

The rock cycle

On Earth's ever-changing surface, rocks are broken down by water and weather, and pieces are moved by glaciers, wind, and water. Those carried to the sea compact into layers of rock. Tectonic activity brings rock to the surface as mid-ocean island chains, mountains, or lava.

Volcanic eruptions create new land through ash and lava deposits.

Snow and rain feed glaciers and streams, which erode rocks.

The remains of marine life and rock pieces compact to form sedimentary rock.

One plate under another causes a volcanic mountain range to form.

Metamorphic rock forms deep inside Earth as a result of heat and pressure.

Roof of the world

Where tectonic plates push together and buckle, mountains grow as rock layers stack on top of one another. The Himalayas (right)—Earth's highest mountains—took shape in the last 50 million years. The range is rising by up to 0.2 in (4 mm) a year, offset by weathering and erosion.

👁 EYEWITNESS

Russell Louis "Rusty" Schweickart
US astronaut Rusty Schweickart's 1969 flight aboard Apollo 9 helped test much of the equipment used on later moon landings. Schweickart (b. 1935) was deeply affected by the sight of Earth from space. He went on to cofound the B612 Foundation, an organization dedicated to protecting the planet from space impacts.

23

Water world

Earth's water makes our planet unique. Oceans and seas of liquid salty water cover about 70 percent of Earth's surface. Fresh water in lakes and rivers, as well as frozen in glaciers, ice sheets, and icebergs, brings the total to more than 80 percent. The movement of water plays a huge role in shaping Earth's surface.

Water cycle
Earth's water moves in a global cycle. The sun's heat warms ocean water, which evaporates into the air. The water vapor rises and condenses into clouds. These release the water as rain and snow. Rain and melted snow and ice flow downhill to the sea, where the cycle starts again.

Amazon River
Rivers hold less than 1 percent of Earth's water but have a big effect on its landscape, carrying about 20 billion tons of sediment to the oceans annually. The Amazon (left) delivers a fifth of all river water reaching the sea.

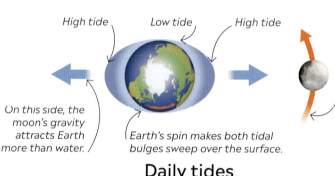

Daily tides
The moon's gravity pulls on the oceans. The pull is stronger nearer to the moon, so a bulge of water forms on the side of Earth nearest to the moon, and on the opposite side. As Earth turns, the bulges create daily changes in the sea level—our high and low tides.

👁 EYEWITNESS

Jacques Piccard
Swiss engineer and oceanographer Jacques Piccard (1922–2008) specialized in designing submersibles. In 1960, alongside US Navy Lieutenant Don Walsh, he made the first descent to the lowest point on Earth, almost 7 miles (11 km) below sea level.

Frozen water
More than three-quarters of Earth's fresh water is ice—in glaciers, ice sheets and shelves (above), icebergs, mountaintop coverings, and soil. Most of it is in the ice sheet covering Antarctica—if it melted, sea levels would rise by about 197 ft (60 m).

The Hawaiian Islands rise 5.9 miles (9.5 km) from the ocean floor.

Hawaii, the largest island in the chain, is five merged volcanoes.

Jason-3 orbits 830 miles (1,336 m) above Earth, passing over the same point every 10 days.

A radar altimeter measures wave height and wind speed.

Water watch
Satellites orbiting Earth monitor its land, oceans, and ice. Jason-3 (above) measures the height of the ocean surface as part of a wider study of changes in sea levels and the effects of climate change. The Aqua satellite studies the water cycle, and CryoSat measures changes in the thickness of the ice sheets.

Under the oceans
The ocean floor is mostly flat plains, but it also has mountains and trenches. The Mariana Trench plunges 7 miles (11 km) below the Pacific Ocean's surface. The Mid-Atlantic Ridge is Earth's longest mountain range. Deep-sea volcanoes that break through the water's surface make islands such as Hawaii.

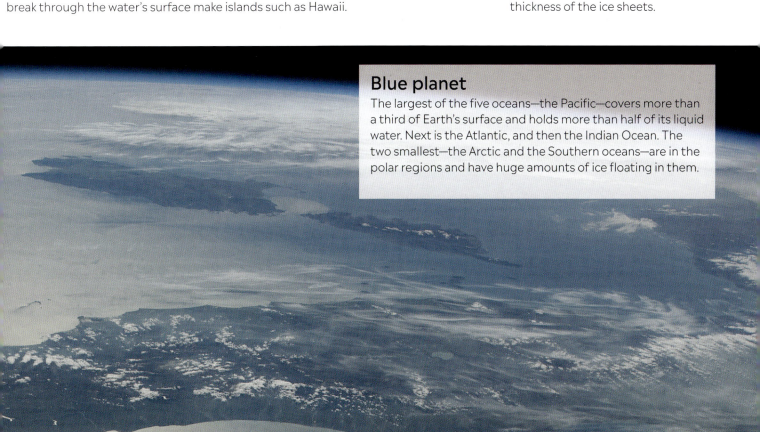

Blue planet
The largest of the five oceans—the Pacific—covers more than a third of Earth's surface and holds more than half of its liquid water. Next is the Atlantic, and then the Indian Ocean. The two smallest—the Arctic and the Southern oceans—are in the polar regions and have huge amounts of ice floating in them.

Living planet

Life began at least 3.7 billion years ago, and evolved from small bacteria-like cells to the huge variety we see today. Human expansion across the planet has contributed to the extinction of other life forms, and to climate change. Yet we are also fascinated by the potential for life on other planets.

Myriad life forms
Earth teems with about 8.7 million species. Each species has its own set of characteristics that suit its own particular environment. There are almost 1 million species of insects, including around 40 species of leafcutter ants (above).

Kingdoms of life
From tiny micro-organisms visible only through a microscope to Earth's largest animals—such as the African elephant (above right)—scientists group the huge variety of life forms into five kingdoms: animals, plants, fungi, protists, and monerans. Monerans are single cells with no internal structure. The protists are single cells but with a nucleus inside. Fungi include yeasts and mushrooms. The most complex life forms are plants and animals.

Beginnings
Life developed from very basic, self-replicating molecules into primitive cells. Multi-cellular organisms gave rise to more complex life such as plants and animals. Stromatolites (right) are layered-rock structures formed by single-cell microbes—similar ones existed on Earth 3.5 billion years ago.

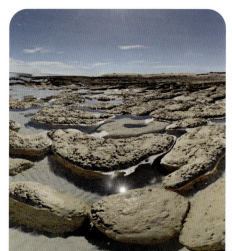

Human impact
Global population growth has led to cutting down forests for farmland, destroying the habitat of thousands of species and reducing the conversion of carbon dioxide to oxygen by trees. As a result, the temperature on Earth increases, polar ice caps melt, and sea levels rise. Tokyo (above) is one of Earth's most populated cities.

Natural selection

Animals born with adaptations that happen to help them in a particular environment thrive and produce more offspring. Over time, this allows their adaptations to spread through an entire population, making it distinct from others. This process, called evolution by natural selection, was first observed by British naturalist Charles Darwin (1809–1882) during a five-year voyage aboard the survey ship HMS *Beagle*.

Extinction

Extinction is a natural part of the evolution of life. Some species adapt and survive events such as climate change or competition from other species, but many die out and become extinct. Many more species are extinct than are alive today.

Lonesome George, the last Pinta Island tortoise, died on June 24, 2012.

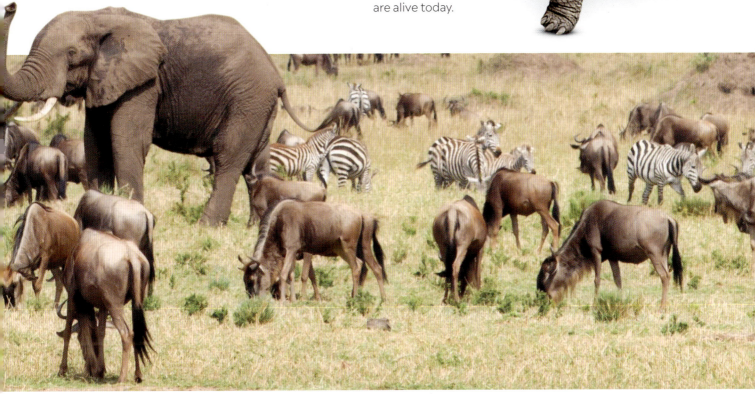

Search for life elsewhere

No evidence of life beyond Earth has yet been found, but spacecraft are searching for life on Mars, and Jupiter's moon Europa is the next target. Beyond the solar system, exoplanets in the habitable zone of their star might harbour life.

Part of the USA's Allen Telescope Array

Extremophiles

Micro-organisms called extremophiles thrive in extreme environments such as scalding and acidic water. Fringing the hot waters of Grand Prismatic Spring (above) in Yellowstone, USA, are orange mats of microbes called archaea, which survive temperatures of up to 165°F (74°C).

The moon

The moon is Earth's nearest neighbor, a quarter of Earth's size, and the largest and brightest object in our night sky. Yet this ball of rock and metal has a dry, dead surface, with huge volcanic plains and highlands covered by impact craters. As it orbits Earth, it appears to change shape, from a slim crescent to a full moon.

Violent origin
About 4.5 billion years ago, a Mars-sized asteroid gave young Earth a glancing blow. Material from both splashed into space, forming a ring around Earth and then slowly clumped together to form the young moon.

Mantle of solid rock
Lower mantle of partially molten rock
Mantle of solid rock
Outer core of molten iron
Crust of solid rock

Inside the moon
Once the moon had formed a ball, it began to cool. Its heavy metals sank as rocks formed its outer layers. Today, the interior has largely solidified around a core of hot iron. The inner core is about 2,600°F (1,400°C), but it is squeezed solid by the rocks around it.

Familiar face
The moon shines by reflected sunlight, and its surface features are easily seen with the naked eye. The near-side face (above) is always turned toward us. Its dark patches are areas of volcanic lava called maria. The lighter areas are older mountainous regions shaped by asteroid impact.

Tycho Crater is about 110 million years old and 53 miles (85 km) across.

28

Waxing crescent

First quarter

Waxing gibbous

Full moon

Waning gibbous

Last quarter

Waning crescent

New moon

Lunar phases
The moon's shape (or phase) appears to change day by day, according to how much of the near side is lit by sunlight. When the moon is between Earth and the sun, its near side is dark (new moon). As it orbits, the moon appears to grow (waxes) until fully lit (full moon) and then shrinks (wanes).

Same face always points to Earth

Day 21

Day 1

Earth

Day 14

Day 7

Direction of moon's orbit

Orbit and rotation
The moon takes 27.3 days to orbit Earth. As it orbits, the moon also spins, taking 27.3 days for one rotation—the same time as one orbit. As a result, the same side of the moon, the near side, shown here in green, always faces Earth.

Lunar eclipse
When Earth is directly between the sun and the moon, it blocks the sunlight. The moon is in Earth's shadow, and is eclipsed. A small amount of sunlight passing around Earth reaches the moon and makes it look reddish.

Ancient landscape
The young moon was bombarded by asteroids, forming craters and pushing up mountains. Volcanism then formed the maria as lava flooded many craters. Little has changed for two billion years except the formation of craters such as Tycho (left).

👁 EYEWITNESS

George Carruthers
US engineer George Carruthers (1939–2020) invented a unique telescope that was used to make some of the first astronomical observations from the moon. His ultraviolet camera and spectrograph, used during the Apollo 16 mission, was designed to capture energies from radiations that are usually blocked out by Earth's atmosphere.

Exploring the moon

People have studied the moon for thousands of years. Since 1959, more than 60 spacecraft have successfully traveled there. Six Apollo missions took 12 men to its surface between 1969 and 1972. It remains the only place that humans have visited beyond Earth.

Galileo and the moon

Italy's Galileo Galilei was the first to study the moon through a telescope. In 1609, he saw that it is not flat, as previously thought, but has mountains, craters, and smoother dark areas. His observations and sketches (such as the lunar phases above) became widely known.

Far side of the moon

In 1959, the Luna 3 spacecraft took the first images of the far side of the moon. Only the Apollo astronauts who have orbited the moon have seen that side in person. China's Chang'e-4 mission landed the first rover on the far side in 2019. The far side is heavily cratered, and because it had less volcanic activity, it has no large maria (lunar plains).

Men on the moon

In the 1960s, American spacecraft were sent to the moon to photograph the surface and soft-land on it. Once a site was chosen for a manned landing, Apollo 11 and its crew blasted off for the moon. Neil Armstrong (far left) and Buzz Aldrin (right) took the first-ever footsteps on the moon, on July 21, 1969, as Michael Collins (center) orbited overhead.

Driving around

The last three Apollo missions—Apollo 15, 16, and 17—used a Lunar Roving Vehicle to explore a wider area. It could carry two astronauts, cameras, tools, and rock and soil samples.

Apollo 17's Eugene Cernan

The rover traveled at up to 11.5 mph (18.5 kph).

Rock and soil

The Apollo astronauts collected 2,200 rock and soil samples weighing a total of 842 lb (382 kg). The breccia rocks (above) formed when asteroid impacts melted and compacted the surface rock and soil. The basalts are volcanic rock formed from lava that seeped through the moon's crust, creating the maria.

Luna landings

The Soviet Union did not land an astronaut on the moon, but it did launch key missions. Luna 9 made the first soft landing there, in 1966, proving that the lunar soil could support landing craft. Luna 16 (featured on stamps, above) was the first to return a soil sample to Earth, in 1970.

Return to the moon

Many spacecraft were sent to the moon in the 1960s and '70s, but none in the 1980s. Recent craft such as the Lunar Reconnaissance Orbiter—orbiting the moon since 1990—carry out scientific research. Japan, Europe, China, and India have sent craft, though the US will likely still be the first to return humans to the moon.

Lunar Reconnaissance Orbiter

Instrument looks for evidence of water as ice

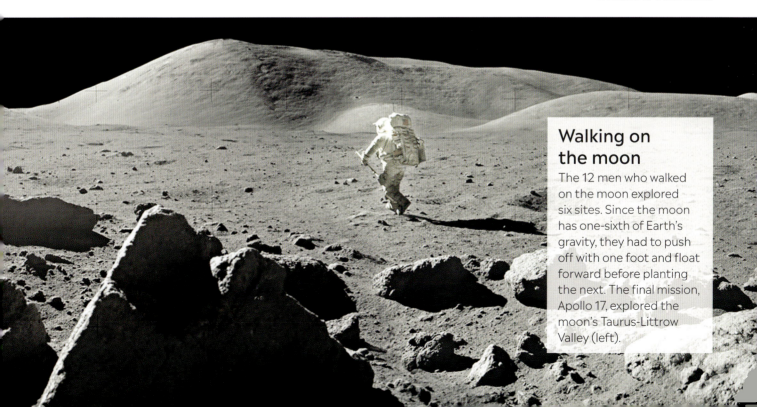

Walking on the moon

The 12 men who walked on the moon explored six sites. Since the moon has one-sixth of Earth's gravity, they had to push off with one foot and float forward before planting the next. The final mission, Apollo 17, explored the moon's Taurus-Littrow Valley (left).

Mars

Fourth from the sun, Mars is the farthest and coldest rocky planet. Its day lasts a little longer than Earth's, it takes 687 days to orbit the sun, and its seasons are all ice-cold. Yet its dry river beds are proof of a much warmer past. Mars is the first planet that humans will visit.

Valles Marineris

Red ball of rock

About half Earth's size, Mars has giant volcanoes and a system of canyons—Valles Marineris—that run a quarter of the way around the equator. Huge valleys carved by rivers in the distant past run north across mainly volcanic plains, and impact craters cover higher terrain to the south.

Water

Mars has water as vapor in its atmosphere and as ice at its poles and below its surface. Channels such as Reull Vallis (right) show that flowing water was once plentiful enough to cut through the landscape.

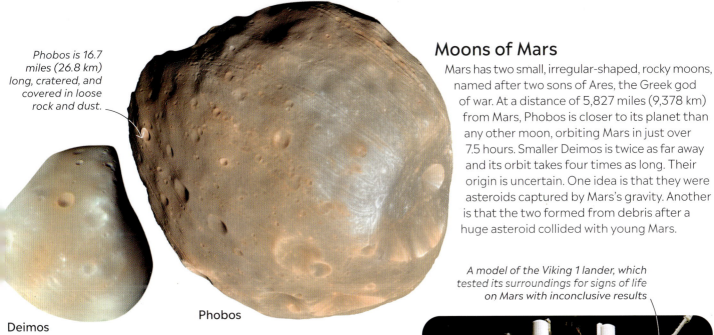

Phobos is 16.7 miles (26.8 km) long, cratered, and covered in loose rock and dust.

Deimos

Phobos

Moons of Mars

Mars has two small, irregular-shaped, rocky moons, named after two sons of Ares, the Greek god of war. At a distance of 5,827 miles (9,378 km) from Mars, Phobos is closer to its planet than any other moon, orbiting Mars in just over 7.5 hours. Smaller Deimos is twice as far away and its orbit takes four times as long. Their origin is uncertain. One idea is that they were asteroids captured by Mars's gravity. Another is that the two formed from debris after a huge asteroid collided with young Mars.

First close-up

Two identical Viking missions arrived at Mars in 1976. Viking 1 transmitted the first black-and-white image from the Martian surface, followed by the first color image (below), revealing a red-colored rocky terrain with fine-grained sand under a red sky.

A model of the Viking 1 lander, which tested its surroundings for signs of life on Mars with inconclusive results

Polar caps

Like Earth, Mars has a white ice cap at each pole. These huge mounds tower over the surrounding landscape. The northern cap is frozen water; the southern is water ice topped by a permanent layer of carbon-dioxide ice. Both caps extend in the winter and shrink in the warmer summer.

Mars's southern cap, named Planum Australe, is about 260 miles (420 km) across in summer.

Putting people on Mars

Space agencies and private companies aim to take people to Mars in the 2030s. Simulated missions on Hawaii (above) keep crews in isolation to see how they might cope on a round trip up to three years long.

33

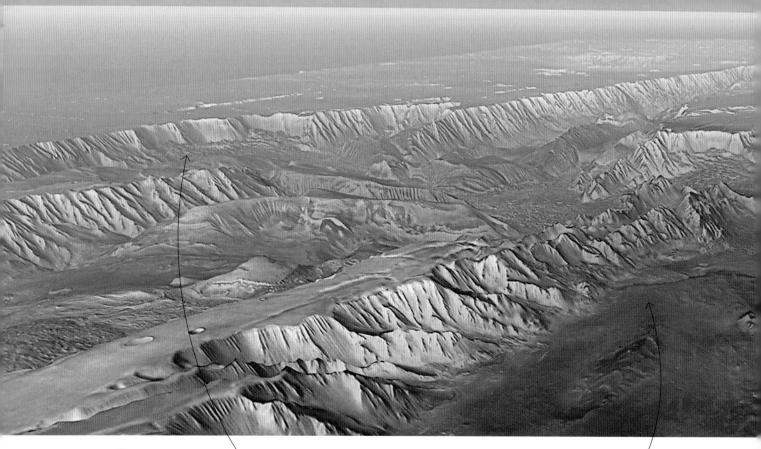

Land has slid down the slopes and collected in the canyon floor.

Melas Chasma is the central and widest part of Valles Marineris.

The Red Planet

Mars is a cold, desert-like world with rock-strewn plains, hills, huge shield volcanoes, and vast canyons. Its rocky crust is in one solid piece over a mantle of rock. When Mars was young, the mantle was warmer and fluid. Its movement tore the crust apart, forming the largest canyons and volcanoes in the solar system.

Blood-red world

Mars's blood-red appearance in our night sky led to it being named after the Roman god of war. The color comes from iron oxide (rust) in the soil that covers almost the entire globe—winds sweep rusty particles up into the thin carbon-dioxide atmosphere.

Olympus Mons

Mars's biggest volcanoes are in the Tharsis Bulge, west of the Valles Marineris. The largest of all, Olympus Mons is 14 miles (22 km) high—almost three times the height of Earth's Mount Everest—and almost as wide as Germany. This huge shield volcano grew gradually as lava flows built up over millions of years.

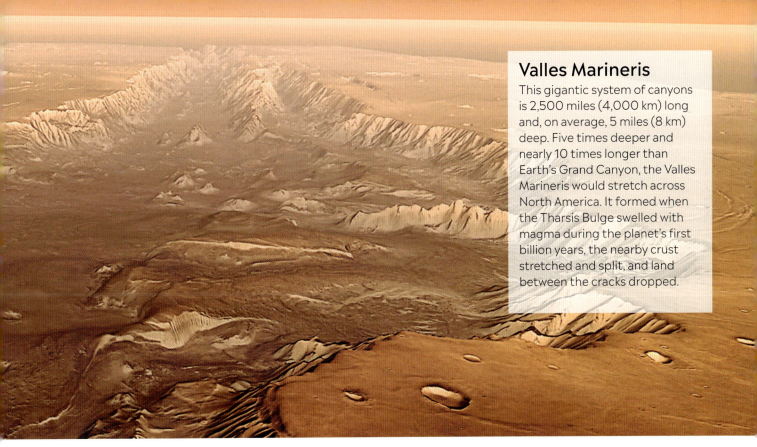

Valles Marineris
This gigantic system of canyons is 2,500 miles (4,000 km) long and, on average, 5 miles (8 km) deep. Five times deeper and nearly 10 times longer than Earth's Grand Canyon, the Valles Marineris would stretch across North America. It formed when the Tharsis Bulge swelled with magma during the planet's first billion years, the nearby crust stretched and split, and land between the cracks dropped.

Fields of dunes
Dunes are common on Mars. They formed as wind piled up the sand and then sculpted it into different shapes. Some look like Earth's dunes, but others have less familiar shapes, such as long straight lines formed by wind consistently blowing in one direction. The crests of these dunes in Endurance Crater are less than 3 ft (1 m) high.

Red sky, blue sunset
Mars's sky is red because of dust particles in the atmosphere. At sunset, the sky around the setting sun turns blue as dust high in the atmosphere scatters sunlight. The rover Spirit captured this sunset in 2005. The Sun is white and smaller than in our sky because Mars is one and a half times farther from the sun than Earth.

Craters within craters
Impact craters are found all over Mars's surface, but especially in its southern regions. Many to the north were covered by lava flows. The largest in this image is Hadley Crater, which is 75 miles (120 km) wide. Lava has flooded its floor, but later impacts each blasted deeper into the surface.

If all the **ice on Mars melted,** water could **cover the planet** to a **depth of 115 ft** (35 m).

35

Roving on Mars

Out of more than 25 successful missions to Mars, 10 have landed on its surface, with six of these roving over the planet's rust-red landscape. Operated by on-board computers directed from Earth, and fitted with cameras and rock-analysis tools, the rovers record their findings and send them back to Earth.

Landing on Mars
Curiosity took just over eight months to travel to Mars, packed inside a protective casing. Lowered to the surface by a descent stage (left), it then cut itself free and the stage flew clear. Previous rovers bounced on to the surface inside a ball of airbags and then drove out.

Curiosity's selfie
Curiosity and Perseverance are the largest and most sophisticated rovers to have explored Mars so far, studying rocks and soil to learn about its past climate and geology, and to find out if it may once have supported life. Curiosity's self-portrait on August 5, 2015, combines several images taken by one of its 17 cameras.

THE ROVERS

The first rover to reach Mars, the US-built Sojourner, explored near its landing site for three months in 1997. The larger twin Mars Exploration Rovers, Spirit and Opportunity, arrived on opposite sides of the planet in 2004. The car-sized Curiosity has been roaming around the planet's surface since its arrival in 2012. It was followed by its near-twin Perseverance, as well as the smaller Chinese rover Zhurong in 2021.

SOJOURNER
July–September 1997
Distance traveled: 330 ft (100 m)

OPPORTUNITY
January 2004–June 2018
Distance traveled: 28.1 miles (45.2 km)

PERSEVERANCE
February 2021–present
Distance traveled: 7.3 miles (11.8 km)

SPIRIT
January 2004–March 2010
Distance traveled: 4.8 miles (7.7 km)

CURIOSITY
August 2012–present
Distance traveled: 17.5 miles (28.2 km)

ZHURONG
May 2021–present
Distance traveled: 1.2 miles (1.9 km)

Drilling into Mars
Spirit and Opportunity scraped samples from surface rocks for study, but Curiosity and Perseverance can extract samples from beneath Mars's surface using drills. The samples are analyzed to find out how the rocks formed, showing evidence of an ancient wet environment.

Flying over Mars
Shortly after landing, Perseverance released a small, four-bladed helicopter called Ingenuity (above). Ingenuity has so far made 32 flights using high-speed rotors to fly in the thin Martian atmosphere. It also helps guide Perseverance and identifies targets for study.

ChemCam's laser emits pulses from here.

The robotic arm, bearing the camera that captured this selfie, is not shown in full in this composite image.

Curiosity's ChemCam
The ChemCam instrument on Curiosity studies rocks and soil from up to 23 ft (7 m) away. Mounted on a mast, it uses a laser to vaporize the target rock surface, while a camera takes images. Another instrument analyzes the light emitted by the rock to determine its composition.

New explorers
Alongside US missions to Mars, other countries are joining the exploration of the Red Planet. China landed its first rover Zhurong in 2021, and the European ExoMars will be the first rover designed particularly to look for signs of past life. Perseverance is also collecting rock samples for return to Earth by a future US–European mission.

EYEWITNESS
Diana Trujillo
After joining NASA, Columbian engineer Diana Trujillo (b.1983) worked on communications for the Curiosity mission and then took charge of the team running the Perseverance rover's robot arm. She is a keen supporter of programs encouraging women and minority groups to enter the space industry.

Investigating Vesta

Vesta is the brightest asteroid in our sky and the only one visible to the naked eye from Earth. Images taken by the spacecraft Dawn in 2011–2012 revealed the scars of collisions with other asteroids. One gouged out a large impact crater near the south pole and sent pieces of Vesta flying. Some landed on Earth, where they were collected as meteorites.

Meteorite evidence

This false-color microscopic view shows various minerals in a 0.2 in (6 mm) wide slice of a meteorite thought to have come from Vesta.

Craters cover Vesta in this view of its northern hemisphere, taken by Dawn in August 2012.

Asteroids

There are millions of asteroids in the solar system, with most in the Asteroid Belt between Mars and Jupiter. Left over from when the planets were forming, these small, rocky bodies follow their own orbits around the sun. The first asteroid to be discovered was Ceres, in 1801. More than 1.1 million asteroids have been identified to date.

SIZE AND SHAPE

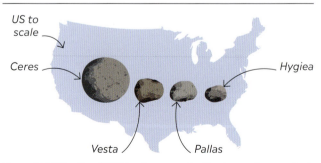

Ceres is 592 miles (952 km) across. As the largest, roundest asteroid, it is also classed as a dwarf planet. Next in size are Vesta, Pallas, and Hygiea. Only 26 asteroids are bigger than 124 miles (200 km) across. Others are irregular in shape and just a few miles wide.

38

Close encounters

Asteroids that come within about 4.7 million miles (7.5 million km) of our planet are potential threats. Hundreds of the larger ones are closely monitored, but small ones arrive unexpectedly. In 2013, an asteroid 59 ft (18 m) wide broke up above Chelyabinsk, Russia, creating a trail of gas and dust (above). Larger chunks fell to the ground as meteorites.

The Asteroid Belt

The asteroids in this doughnut-shaped ring typically take four to five years to orbit the sun. Once the orbit of a newly found asteroid is known, the body may be assigned a name chosen by the discoverer. There are also two swarms of asteroids that have similar orbits to Jupiter and are named the Trojans.

Down to Earth

Tons of asteroid material reach Earth every day. Much of it is in the form of small pieces that burn up in the atmosphere. Pieces too large to burn up reach the surface and are called meteorites. Each year, around 3,000 meteorites weighing more than 2.2 lb (1 kg) land on Earth.

A meteorite weighing 2.25 tons (2,045 kg) was found in Saudi Arabia's Empty Quarter in 1966.

Impact with Earth

Large asteroid impacts on Earth are very rare. An asteroid at least 492 ft (150 m) wide strikes Earth roughly every 10,000 years and would produce a crater about 1.5 miles (2.5 km) wide. One of Earth's 190 impact craters, Pingualuit Crater in Canada (above), is the result of an impact around 1.4 million years ago. It is 2.1 miles (3.4 km) across.

Studied by spacecraft

The first dedicated mission to an asteroid was NEAR Shoemaker, which landed on Eros in 2001. Hayabusa (left) collected dust from Itokawa in 2005 and sent it back to Earth. In 2020, the OSIRIS-REx mission collected rock from the asteroid Bennu for return to Earth.

Jupiter

The solar system's largest and most massive planet is named after the king of the Roman gods and ruler of the sky. Five times the distance of Earth from the sun, and the closest giant planet, Jupiter is made of mainly hydrogen and helium, with no solid surface. When we look at it, we see only the top of its deep atmosphere.

Giant world

Jupiter is made of almost two and a half times the material of the other seven planets combined, and 11 Earths would fit across its face. Yet it is the fastest spinner of all the planets, turning once in less than 10 hours. Its rapid rotation, fierce winds, and the large-scale movement of gases create the stripes that run parallel to its equator.

The Great Red Spot is the largest storm in the solar system.

COLORED CLOUDS

- *Winds sweep high clouds into bands.*
- *High clouds are colder and paler.*
- *Low clouds are warmer and darker.*
- *Warm gases rise, cool, and then sink.*
- *Water clouds form deeper in the atmosphere.*

Hydrogen gas dominates Jupiter's atmosphere. The rest is mostly helium, with small amounts of hydrogen compounds that form the colorful bands of clouds at different heights. Warm gases rising from the lower, darker bands (called belts) form high, icy clouds in the paler bands (zones), then cool and sink in a constant cycle.

Comet crashes

Jupiter's gravitational pull can change the orbit of a passing asteroid, distort a moon's shape, or break up a comet. When comet Shoemaker-Levy was pulled into orbit around Jupiter, it was soon torn into 21 pieces that smashed into the planet's atmosphere in July 1994. Since then, short-lived bruises from several other comet crashes have been spotted in Jupiter's clouds.

Magnetic field

Jupiter has a magnetic field generated by electric currents within its body. This field influences a huge region of space around the planet. Solar wind particles and others from Jupiter's moon Io are drawn into the upper atmosphere above the poles, creating light displays called auroras.

Jupiter's auroras are hundreds of times brighter than Earth's.

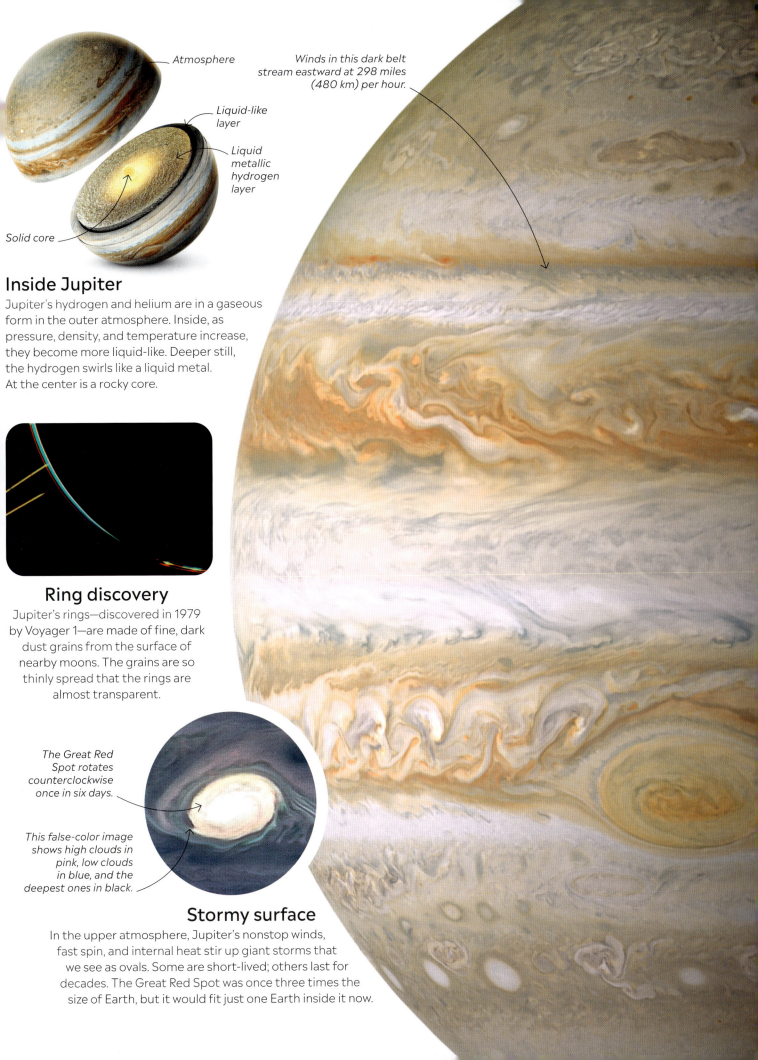

- Atmosphere
- Liquid-like layer
- Liquid metallic hydrogen layer
- Solid core

Inside Jupiter

Jupiter's hydrogen and helium are in a gaseous form in the outer atmosphere. Inside, as pressure, density, and temperature increase, they become more liquid-like. Deeper still, the hydrogen swirls like a liquid metal. At the center is a rocky core.

Ring discovery

Jupiter's rings—discovered in 1979 by Voyager 1—are made of fine, dark dust grains from the surface of nearby moons. The grains are so thinly spread that the rings are almost transparent.

Winds in this dark belt stream eastward at 298 miles (480 km) per hour.

The Great Red Spot rotates counterclockwise once in six days.

This false-color image shows high clouds in pink, low clouds in blue, and the deepest ones in black.

Stormy surface

In the upper atmosphere, Jupiter's nonstop winds, fast spin, and internal heat stir up giant storms that we see as ovals. Some are short-lived; others last for decades. The Great Red Spot was once three times the size of Earth, but it would fit just one Earth inside it now.

Jupiter's moons

Jupiter is orbited by at least 80 moons and astronomers are on the lookout for more. The largest four are huge, round worlds in their own right, each with complex surface features. About a dozen are tens of miles across, and the rest are just a few miles wide and irregular in shape.

First discovery
Italy's Galileo Galilei was the first to see Jupiter's four largest moons, in 1610. They were the first moons to be found after Earth's moon and are known as the Galileans. Galileo's portrait and his description of a 1610 observation are on the Juno spacecraft now at Jupiter.

White areas appear where impact craters expose new ice

Ganymede

Callisto's surface is the most heavily cratered in the solar system.

Callisto

The Galilean moons
Ganymede, Callisto, Io, and Europa are known as the Galilean moons. Ganymede is bigger than the planet Mercury and is the largest moon in the solar system. It is an icy world—so too are Callisto and Europa. Io is the closest of the four to Jupiter and is covered in volcanoes. Jupiter's gravity distorts Io's shape and generates internal heat that is released at the moon's surface.

Ganymede's icy surface
Ganymede has an icy crust of bright and dark areas—the bright regions are mostly ice-tipped ridges and grooves, the dark ones, impact craters. Enki Catena, a chain of 13 craters that runs between the two areas, formed as fragments of an asteroid or comet crashed into the moon.

Ice-filled cracks called linea criss-cross Europa's surface.
Solid crust of ice
Warm ice layer
Liquid water ocean is about 62 miles (100 km) deep

Europa and water

The smallest and second-most distant of the Galilean moons, Europa is squeezed and stretched by the gravitational pull of Jupiter on one side and Ganymede on the other. An ocean of liquid water beneath its frozen crust is one of the few places in the solar system that could be hospitable to life. Ganymede also has an ocean, roughly 124 miles (200 km) below its surface, between layers of ice.

Volcanic Io

In 1979, US astronomer Linda Morabito (b.1953) was studying images of Io from the Voyager 1 mission when she spotted a crescent of light above the moon's edge. She soon proved this was due to a volcanic eruption on Io.

Triple eclipse

Jupiter's largest moons regularly travel across its face, but the sight of three at a time occurs only once or twice a decade. In this view by the Hubble Space Telescope in January 2015, Callisto, Europa, and Io are all passing between Jupiter and the sun, casting shadows on the planet as they eclipse the sun.

Callisto | Europa's shadow | Callisto's shadow | Io | Io's shadow

Io is covered by lava flows, and towering plumes of molten sulfur burst from its volcanic craters.

Io

Europa

Io's tallest mountain, Boösaule Montes, is twice the height of Mount Everest at 57,415 ft (17,500 m) high.

21st-century discoveries

Many small moons have been discovered since 1610, and those identified since 2000 are smaller still. More than 50 have been detected by a team led by Scott S. Sheppard at the Mauna Kea Observatory in Hawaii (right). Averaging 1.9 miles (3 km) across, they orbit clockwise in the opposite direction to the Galileans, which suggests they are captured asteroids.

Saturn

In ancient times, Saturn was the most distant planet known, and marked the edge of the solar system. We now know this giant planet is the second largest, the sixth of eight orbiting the sun, with a wide system of rings and a large family of moons. The Cassini probe orbited Saturn from 2004 until 2017.

Early observations

When Galileo Galilei used his telescope to observe Saturn in 1610, he noted its strange shape. Galileo thought the planet might be flanked by two huge moons, while others suggested it had handle-like extensions or an oval shape with dark spots. Dutch astronomer Christiaan Huygens was the first to explain the true nature of the rings in the 1650s. His drawings of Saturn from his book *Systema Saturnium* (1659) are shown above.

Horizontal winds sweep the colored clouds into bands like those on Jupiter, but with fewer storms.

Ringed world

Like Jupiter, Saturn is mainly hydrogen and helium, gaseous in its outer layer but liquid inside. Not quite as wide as Jupiter, it has less than a third of its material, making Saturn the least dense of all the planets. It is also the least spherical; its low density and fast spin of less than 11 hours fling its equatorial regions out to form a bulging waist.

The Cassini Division looks empty from Earth but is full of ring material.

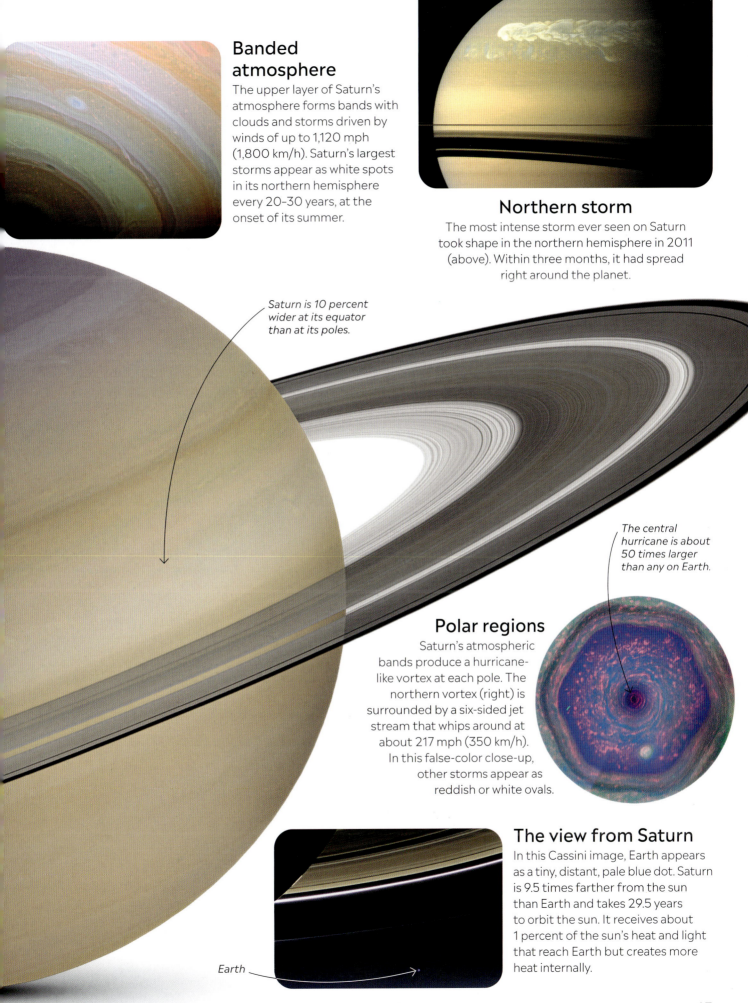

Banded atmosphere

The upper layer of Saturn's atmosphere forms bands with clouds and storms driven by winds of up to 1,120 mph (1,800 km/h). Saturn's largest storms appear as white spots in its northern hemisphere every 20–30 years, at the onset of its summer.

Northern storm

The most intense storm ever seen on Saturn took shape in the northern hemisphere in 2011 (above). Within three months, it had spread right around the planet.

Saturn is 10 percent wider at its equator than at its poles.

The central hurricane is about 50 times larger than any on Earth.

Polar regions

Saturn's atmospheric bands produce a hurricane-like vortex at each pole. The northern vortex (right) is surrounded by a six-sided jet stream that whips around at about 217 mph (350 km/h). In this false-color close-up, other storms appear as reddish or white ovals.

The view from Saturn

In this Cassini image, Earth appears as a tiny, distant, pale blue dot. Saturn is 9.5 times farther from the sun than Earth and takes 29.5 years to orbit the sun. It receives about 1 percent of the sun's heat and light that reach Earth but creates more heat internally.

Earth

Saturn's rings

The most impressive rings of any planet encircle Saturn. They are made of millions of orbiting pieces prevented by Saturn's gravity from combining to form a single moon. The rings extend to many times Saturn's width but average only about 33 ft (10 m) deep, and small moons sweep the gaps in between.

EYEWITNESS

Giovanni Cassini
Italian-born Cassini (1625–1712), the first director of the Paris Observatory, France, was one of the first to observe Saturn. In 1675, he spotted the gap dividing the A and B rings that now bears his name. He also discovered four moons: Iapetus, Rhea, Tethys, and Dione.

D ring — C ring — B ring — Cassini Division — A ring — F ring

Keeler Gap

Rings within rings
The rings most readily seen from Earth are named A, B, and C. Each consists of individual rings of material. At either side of these three are more recently discovered rings that are almost transparent. The D ring is closest to Saturn, while E, F, and G lie beyond the A ring. There are a small number of gaps between the rings, such as the Cassini Division. They look empty from a distance but are full of material.

Icy particles reflect sunlight well, making the rings bright and easy to see.

Ring pieces
The pieces that make up the rings are dusty water ice, and range in size from tiny grains to truck-sized boulders. Each follows its own circular orbit in a plane extending out from Saturn's equator. Their origin is uncertain. The pieces could be debris from a moon torn apart by Saturn's gravity, or from a moon destroyed in a collision with another body.

November 2000

November 1999

October 1998

October 1997

October 1996

Changing view
Our view of the rings changes as Saturn orbits the sun. The planet tilts by 27 degrees on its spin axis, and each hemisphere points toward the sun once per orbit. In these five views, more and more of the southern hemisphere faces the sun. The rings will lie edge on in 2025, and be wide open once again in 2032.

Ring peaks
The gravity of moons within the ring system causes kinks and waves in individual rings, or forces pieces into peaks. Cassini imaged these peaks rising up to 1.6 miles (2.5 km) above the edge of the B ring.

Tall peaks cast long shadows on the B ring.

Shepherd moon
Daphnis (right) is just 5 miles (8 km) wide and orbits within the Keeler Gap. It shepherds material into the ring and maintains the gap, causing ripples on both edges.

Giant dust ring
A huge new ring found in 2009 is tilted from Saturn's main ring system. Made of dust, it starts 3.7 million miles (6 million km) from Saturn and extends twice as far again. It is also very thick, about 20 times Saturn's width from top to bottom. Invisible to the eye, the giant ring is seen here in infrared.

Saturn's moons

Saturn's 83 moons range from Titan, bigger than Mercury, to more than 30 city-sized icy rocks. The planet has seven major moons, all of which are round. The bigger ones orbit closest to Saturn—some within its rings—while the smallest orbit up to 15.5 million miles (25 million km) away. All are icy worlds, but Titan is the only solar system moon with a dense atmosphere and liquid seas and lakes.

EYEWITNESS

Christiaan Huygens
Dutch astronomer Christiaan Huygens (1629–1695) made advances in telescope design that allowed him to discover Saturn's moon Titan in 1655, and to figure out the true structure of Saturn's rings. His other important breakthroughs include the invention of the pendulum clock.

Explosive Enceladus
When NASA's space probe Cassini flew by Enceladus, it saw that huge areas have been resurfaced and that it is geologically active. Jets of water ice and water vapor burst through four long fractures in its crust and into nearby space. The water comes from subsurface lakes that could support life.

Hyperion
Some of Saturn's moons are irregular in shape. Hyperion, the largest of these, is 360 km (224 miles) long. This icy rock body looks spongelike—hit by other objects in the past, its surface material was blasted away. It orbits Saturn in 21.3 days, rotating chaotically as it travels.

Ithaca Chasma is a canyon system that runs for 757 miles (1,219 km).

Herschel Crater is named after William Herschel, who discovered Mimas.

Long fractures cut through the icy surface.

Mimas
The innermost and smallest of Saturn's major moons orbits in the Cassini Division.

Enceladus
This bright moon orbits within the E ring, beyond the main rings. It is 318 miles (512 km) across.

Tethys
Like Mimas and Enceladus, Tethys is made of water-ice and rock. It shares its orbit with two small, irregular-shaped moons.

Dione
Long, white streaks on Dione's cratered surface are deep canyons in the icy crust. Dione orbits within the E ring, with two small, irregular moons.

Seas on Titan

Titan's three large seas are all close to the north pole. Ligeia Mare (above) is the second largest, and contains mainly methane. It is about 311 miles (500 km) at its widest point, and up to 525 ft (160 m) deep.

Titan

The second-largest moon in the solar system is a cold world of rock and ice about 3,200 miles (5,150 km) across, hidden by a thick nitrogen atmosphere. Cassini's instruments revealed Titan's surface for the first time, showing a world where low temperatures create a methane cycle similar to Earth's water cycle.

Huygens probe

Cassini's Huygens probe parachuted on to Titan's surface and sent back data for about 90 minutes. The landing site was flat and strewn with smooth pebbles and rocks.

Engelier Crater

Bright icy material thrown out by an impact crater

Iapetus

Iapetus takes 79.3 days to orbit, at an average distance of 2.2 million miles (3.6 million km) from Saturn. One side is dark, the other light, with craters on both—Engelier, one of the largest, is 313 miles (504 km) wide.

Rhea

Rhea is Saturn's second-largest moon—949 miles (1,528 km) across—and the first of the moons that orbit Saturn beyond the ring system, completing its orbit in 4.5 days. Rhea's icy surface is heavily pockmarked by impact craters.

49

Where are they now?

All four Pioneer and Voyager craft continue to travel away from the sun. The year of launch, and the year and distance when we last received a signal from Pioneer 10 and 11, are shown above. The Voyagers are still sending signals from beyond the planets.

PIONEER 11
(1973–1995)
4 billion miles
(6.5 billion km)

PIONEER 10
(1972–2003)
7.6 billion miles
(12.2 billion km)

Visiting the giants

The first spacecraft to venture beyond the Asteroid Belt and fly by the outer planets were Pioneer 10 and 11 and Voyager 1 and 2, which were launched in the 1970s. In-depth study came later, with Galileo and Juno, and Cassini orbiting Jupiter and Saturn, respectively.

Message from Earth
While the Pioneers carried a metal plaque identifying their origin, the Voyagers have a gramophone record that locates Earth and includes many of its sounds and images. Information on the cover (left) is designed to enable any advanced civilization to play the record.

Graphics show how to play the record.

The grand tour
Voyager 2 launch August 20, 1977
Voyager 1 launch September 5, 1977

The Voyager craft left Earth in 1977. Voyager 1 flew by Jupiter and Saturn and was the first to leave the planetary part of the solar system when it entered interstellar space in 2012. Voyager 2 flew past Jupiter and Saturn and then past Uranus and Neptune. By harnessing the gravity of each planet, it swung from one to the next, using less fuel.

Sunshield
High-gain antenna for communication with Earth

Galileo at Jupiter
In 1995–2003, Galileo (above) made the first long-term study of Jupiter in close-up, with 35 orbits of the planet and flybys of its Galilean moons. It also released a probe into Jupiter's atmosphere. At the end of the mission, it destroyed itself by plunging into Jupiter to avoid contaminating its moons.

👁 EYEWITNESS

Carl Sagan
US astronomer Carl Sagan (1934–1996) was involved in several of NASA's early space probes. Knowing that Pioneer 10 and 11 and Voyager 1 and 2 would continue traveling far beyond the solar system, he devised metal panels and records to carry messages to alien civilizations.

Cassini's main radio dish is 4 m (13 ft) across.

VOYAGER 2	VOYAGER 1
(1977–ongoing)	(1977–ongoing)
12.1 billion miles	14.6 billion miles
(19.5 billion km)	(23.5 billion km)

Cassini's mission to Saturn

The size of a bus, Cassini is the largest and most complex craft sent to a planet. In 2004, it started orbiting Saturn (below). On an early flyby of Titan, it released the Huygens probe on to the moon's surface. Its mission ended in 2017, after 20 years of service—7 traveling to Saturn and 13 in orbit.

Cassini recorded ring particles and temperature as it orbited Saturn.

Holes in the probe's cover let in atmospheric gas for analysis.

Huygens' descent to Titan

On release by Cassini, Huygens' main parachute opened to slow its descent to Titan. As its heat shield fell away, the probe began to test the atmosphere and image the moon's surface. It transmitted data as it fell and for about 1.5 hours after landing.

A closer look

The Juno mission arrived at Jupiter in 2016, entering a highly elongated orbit that flies within 2,600 miles (4,200 km) of the planet's poles. This allows it to study Jupiter's magnetic and gravitational fields, while reducing the damage from belts of radiation near its equator.

The outer solar system

The first object discovered beyond Saturn was Uranus, in 1781. Today, we know the dark and cold outer region of the solar system contains billions of objects—not only the planets Uranus and Neptune but dwarf planets and a ring of Kuiper Belt objects, too. Beyond, surrounding all of this, lies the Oort Cloud of deep-frozen comet nuclei.

The Kuiper Belt is 30–50 times farther from the sun than Earth is.

The Oort Cloud consists of billions of comet nuclei on individual orbits around the sun.

The sun and the planets are in the center of the Oort Cloud.

The Oort Cloud
The vast Oort Cloud is a reservoir of comet nuclei that follow elongated paths around the sun in all directions. As a group, they form the spherical Oort Cloud, which surrounds the rest of the solar system. The outer edge of the cloud is about 100,000 times more distant from the sun than Earth is and stretches halfway to the nearest stars.

Beyond Saturn
The eight planets orbit the sun in roughly the same plane, making a disc-shaped system. Beyond is the Kuiper Belt, a flattened belt thought to contain hundreds of thousands of ice-and-rock bodies. Many of these, such as Pluto, follow orbits that take them out of the planetary plane. The Belt and the Oort Cloud are made up of material left over after the planets formed at the dawn of the solar system.

Planet discovery
William Herschel (left) was a German-born astronomer. When he found Uranus in 1781, no one knew planets existed beyond Saturn. Scientists then realized that something was pulling on Uranus as it orbited the sun and predicted the likely location of a more distant planet. In 1846, German astronomer Johann Galle discovered Neptune.

Kuiper Belt objects
More than 2,000 ice-and-rock bodies are known in the Kuiper Belt. Most are classed as Kuiper Belt objects (KBOs), some are comet nuclei, and the largest are dwarf planets such as Pluto. In 2019, the New Horizons probe sent back close-up views of a KBO called Arrokoth (above). They showed that it was made of two smaller objects that had gently collided and had a reddish surface due to long exposure to the sun's weak radiation.

Makemake is about 889 miles (1,430 km) across and has a moon.

What's in a name?

Some astronomers refer to the Kuiper Belt and Oort Cloud as the Edgeworth-Kuiper Belt and Öpik-Oort Cloud. Kenneth Edgeworth predicted a belt in 1943—in 1951, Gerard Kuiper came up with a similar idea. Ernst Öpik suggested the cloud of comets in 1932. Jan Oort (right) revived the idea in the 1950s.

Dwarf planets

The first solar system body known beyond Neptune was Pluto. Classed as a planet after its discovery in 1930, Pluto differed from the others in size, makeup, and orbit, and has a huge moon, Charon. Pluto is now classed as one of four dwarf planets in the Kuiper Belt. The others are Eris, Haumea, and Makemake (above).

Charon

Pluto

Artist's impression of the view from Sedna

Most distant

Some objects follow orbits out beyond the Kuiper Belt. Like Eris, they could be dwarf planets, or also be the first inner Oort Cloud objects to be found. Sedna (left) is 90 times the Earth–sun distance. The farthest known is 2018AG37, at more than 132 times the Earth–sun distance.

53

Uranus

Barely visible to the naked eye, and twice as far from the sun as its inner neighbor Saturn, Uranus is a freezing cold world. Only Voyager 2 has visited this ice giant, flying by in 1986. Spinning on its side as it makes its 84-year orbit of the sun, Uranus has faint, dark rings and 27 moons, which are much smaller than Earth's moon.

Some parts of Uranus's atmosphere are –371°F (–224°C) colder than any other planet.

Pale blue ball
Uranus is four times the width of Earth and is the solar system's third-largest planet. It is made mainly of water, ammonia, and methane. They form a slushy liquid mantle around a core of molten iron and magma. The outer layer is an atmosphere of hydrogen and helium. Methane gas in the atmosphere absorbs the red wavelengths of incoming sunlight and gives Uranus its blue coloring.

Clouds appear white, and pink around the planet's edge represents a high-altitude haze.

Bright clouds
When Voyager 2 flew by, the south pole faced the sun and the planet looked featureless. But when the equator faces the sun, new parts of Uranus are warmed up and it becomes a dynamic world. Infrared imaging (left) highlights its banded structure and bright clouds.

Tilted planet
Uranus's spin axis is tilted at almost right angles to its orbit, so it rolls along its path like a ball. Its rings and moons seem to orbit it from top to bottom. During the planet's orbit, each pole points once to the sun, receiving 42 years of sunlight, followed by 42 years of darkness.

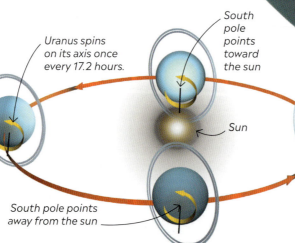

Uranus spins on its axis once every 17.2 hours.

South pole points toward the sun

Sun

South pole points away from the sun

Equator faces the sun

The inner rings consist of dust and dark, rocky material from a few centimeters to several feet across.

Inner and outer rings

Uranus has 13 narrow rings made of dust and dark, rocky material—11 form an inner ring system, and two are more distant. In this false-color image of the inner rings, the bright white one is Epsilon, the farthest from Uranus. Closer and thinner rings, just a few miles across, are pale green, pale blue, and cream.

EYEWITNESS

Gerard Kuiper

Uranus's fifth moon Miranda was discovered in 1948 by Dutch astronomer Gerard Kuiper (1905–1973), who also made several other important planetary discoveries. He was the first to detect carbon dioxide in the atmosphere of Mars, and the belt of icy objects beyond Neptune is named after him.

Moons

Only Uranus's five largest moons are roughly spherical. From largest to smallest, they are Titania, Oberon, Umbriel, Ariel, and Miranda. The other 22 are smaller and irregular in shape. The closest orbit Uranus in just hours, while the five largest take between one and 13 days, and the farthest take years. Tiny Puck, just 101 miles (162 km) across, orbits in 18 hours.

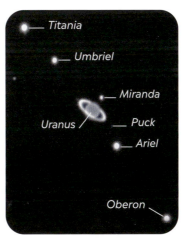

Clouds of ammonia, frozen methane, and frozen water droplets in the atmosphere

Titania

The largest of Uranus's moons, Titania is just under half the size of Earth's moon. Its icy surface is marked by impact craters and long canyon systems—cracks that formed when the young moon expanded.

Gertrude Crater is Titania's largest.

Miranda

The smallest, innermost of the major moons is crisscrossed by ridges and canyons, and has the solar system's tallest cliff. Verona Rupes (above) is almost 6 miles (10 km) high. Some think it formed when the moon split apart after a colossal collision and came together again.

Adams ring is Neptune's outermost ring

Neptune's rings are so thin and sparse that they appear transparent to the eye.

Neptune

The most distant planet in the solar system, Neptune is 30 times farther from the sun than Earth. It was also the last to be discovered, in 1846, and the last to be visited by a spacecraft, Voyager 2 in 1989. Neptune has the longest orbital path around the sun, completing just one 165-year orbit since its discovery.

Deep blue world

Neptune is an ice giant like Uranus and is made of mainly water, ammonia, and methane. Beneath its atmosphere is a slushy layer of liquid and ice, and deep inside is a core of rock and iron. It is a little smaller than Uranus but more massive, due to its thinner atmosphere and deeper liquid layer. Its spin axis is tilted at a similar angle to Earth's, and it experiences seasons – each lasting about 40 years.

Atmosphere

Neptune's atmosphere is mainly hydrogen and helium, with water, ammonia, and methane increasing with depth. Fast winds whip around the planet at up to 1,300 mph (2,100 km/h), 10 times faster than hurricanes on Earth, and clouds sporadically appear.

Dark spot with white clouds above it

Dark spots

Huge storms on Neptune appear as dark spots. The Great Dark Spot—seen by Voyager 2 in 1989—was almost as big as Earth, but disappeared a few years later. A spot the size of the United States appeared in May 2016 (left, captured by the Hubble Space Telescope).

Methane ice strongly reflects heat radiation seen by JWST

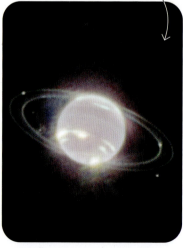

Neptune's rings and storms, as seen by the James Webb Space Telescope (JWST)

Rings

Neptune's five dark, dusty rings are difficult to see except when lit by the sun from behind. Their presence had been predicted, but it was Voyager 2's flyby that confirmed the rings' existence. It also found the moon Despina, shepherding particles in the Le Verrier ring, and Galatea, which shepherds particles in the brighter outer Adams ring.

Triton
About three-quarters the size of our moon, Triton is a ball of rock and ice and orbits Neptune in less than six days. Its surface temperature of –391°F (–235°C) is one of the coldest in the solar system. Pink methane ice is found near its south pole (right).

Plumes of nitrogen gas and dust reach 5 miles (8 km) above Triton's surface.

Ice volcanism
Triton is ice-cold but volcanically active. Voyager 2's images of the surface revealed smooth plains of volcanic ice, and mounds and pits formed by icy lava. Beneath is a mantle of ice that erupts through surface cracks. Heated by the sun, the nitrogen ice turns to gas, and plumes of gas and dust jet up high above the surface.

Methane gas in the atmosphere absorbs red wavelengths in sunlight, giving Neptune its blue color.

Moons
Neptune's 14 moons are mostly small and irregular, but Triton is spherical and 1,682 miles (2,707 km) wide. It was discovered in 1846, just a couple of weeks after Neptune, but no others were found until Nereid, in 1949. The latest and smallest, Hippocamp, was discovered in 2013 by the Hubble Space Telescope.

Methane ice clouds in the atmosphere change their appearance in hours.

Hippocamp · Psamathe · Laomedeia · Sao · Neso · Halimede · Naiad · Thalassa · Despina · Galatea · Larissa · Nereid · Proteus · Triton

The outer dwarfs

Four known dwarf planets orbit in the Kuiper Belt. Pluto was discovered in 1930 during the search for a ninth major planet, while the others were found among the Kuiper Belt Objects in the early 2000s. All four are small, cold worlds of ice and rock. New Horizons revealed more detail when it flew by Pluto in 2015.

Seeing Pluto close up
New Horizons' images of Pluto showed mountains as high as Earth's Rockies, and the solar system's largest glacier—the crater-free, central region called Sputnik Planitia. This 620-mile (1,000 km) wide ice plain is constantly renewed as older nitrogen ice is replaced by newer material rising from underneath.

Clyde Tombaugh with his own reflecting telescope in 1928

Discovery
American astronomer Clyde Tombaugh joined the Lowell Observatory in Arizona, in 1929. In a search for the ninth planet (Planet X), he took photos of the same region of sky on different nights and compared the images to identify objects that had moved. In February 1930, he found the object later named Pluto.

Mountains capped with methane snow and ice, in the dark Cthulu Regio

Norgay Montes—ice mountains up to 2.2 miles (3.5 km) high—captured by New Horizons in July 2015

Sputnik Planitia

Frozen landscape
Pluto has snowcapped mountain ranges, ice plains, vast canyons, and craters formed by impacts with other Kuiper Belt bodies. During Pluto's 248-year orbit, its thin nitrogen atmosphere freezes to ice and snow and then evaporates again with the changing seasons.

Thin crust mainly of frozen nitrogen

Inside Pluto

Pluto's huge rocky core accounts for about 60 percent of the dwarf planet's entire mass. The core is surrounded by a mantle of water ice, which may include a water ice ocean. The thin crust is made mostly of frozen nitrogen, as well as water, carbon dioxide, and methane.

Mantle of water ice
Core of silicate rock

SMALL WORLD

Pluto is only 1,473 miles (2,370 km) wide—far less than the width of the US. Pluto's moon Charon is a little more than half of Pluto's size, which suggests the two were formed at the same time, from the same material.

Pluto *Charon*

A nuclear generator powered New Horizons' instruments at Pluto.

New Horizons

After a journey of more than 3 billion miles (4.8 billion km), New Horizons flew by Pluto on July 14, 2015. The spacecraft sent back hundreds of images of Pluto and its moons. In 2019, the probe sent back data from its close encounter with a Kuiper Belt Object called Arrokoth.

Sputnik Planitia is the western, smoother side of the heart-shaped Tombaugh Regio.

Dwarfs and moons

Eris and Makemake have one moon each, Haumea has two, and Pluto has five. Charon, discovered in 1978, is Pluto's closest moon. The four smaller ones were found in 2005-2012, using the Hubble Space Telescope. This artist's view shows Eris, its small moon, Dysnomia, above it, and the distant sun (top left).

Dysnomia *Eris*

Makemake Haumea Pluto Eris

The four outer dwarfs

Pluto was discovered in 1930, Haumea in 2004, and Eris and Makemake in 2005. Each has enough mass to be almost spherical but has not cleared its orbital path of other objects.

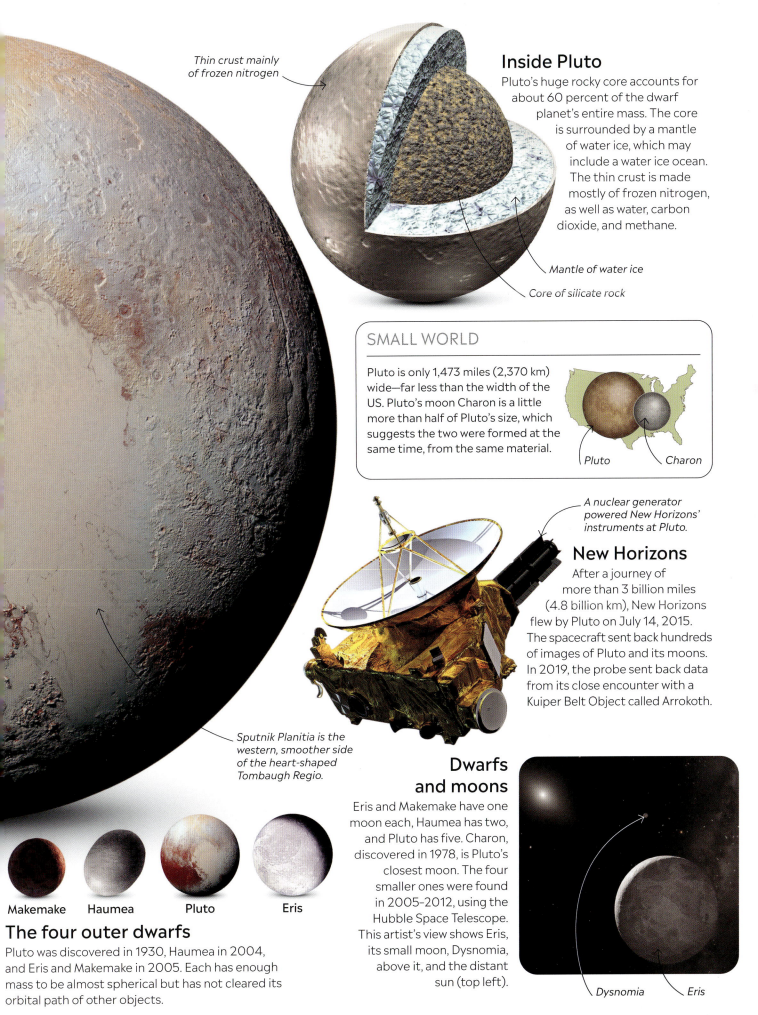

59

Comets

This illustration of a comet nucleus reveals the snow, ice, and rock dust held together loosely by gravity.

Visitors from the edge of the solar system, comets are primitive material left over from when the planets formed. These city-sized, dirty snowballs, each on its own orbit around the sun, are mostly too distant to be seen. Every so often, when a star's gravity pushes one much closer to the sun, it becomes a long-tailed comet.

👁 EYEWITNESS

Caroline Herschel
German astronomer Caroline Herschel (1750–1848), sister of William Herschel (discoverer of Uranus), was one of the first women to have her work recognized by the scientific community in Europe. She discovered at least five comets.

Dirty snowball nucleus

In the 1950s, American Fred Whipple suggested that the long-tailed comets we see in our skies are produced by a huge, dirty snowball nucleus. In 1986, the Giotto spacecraft imaged the nucleus of Comet Halley. It was a mix of two-thirds snow and ice, one-third rock-dust, 9.5 miles (15.3 km) in length.

The surface loses a layer 3.3 ft (1 m) thick on each close orbit to the sun.

Great comets

About 10 comets a century are bright enough to be easily seen in the night sky and are classed as great comets. Historically, they were named for the year they appeared. Today, they take their discoverer's name. The brightest one so far this century was Comet McNaught in 2007 (above).

Periodic comets

Some comets follow orbits that bring them back time and again to Earth's sky and are called periodic comets. Halley reappears about every 76 years. It shines above the nativity scene in *The Adoration of the Magi* (right), painted by Italian artist Giotto di Bondone in about 1305.

60

TOWARD THE SUN

A comet becomes big and bright only as it orbits closer to the sun. The sun's heat turns its snow and ice to gas, which jets out from the nucleus, taking dust with it. A huge coma (head) forms around the nucleus, and two tails—one of gas, the other, dust. They shrink again as it moves away.

- The comet grows two tails, usually millions of miles long.
- Sun
- The tails shrink as the comet moves away from the sun.
- Gas tail
- Dust tail

Discovery

The SOHO spacecraft has recorded more than 3,000 comets passing close by the sun. Using a filter tool to block the sun's bright light (black and red, left) reveals a comet's faint light.

Comet ISON, discovered by telescope, swings around the sun in this SOHO image from 2013.

Spacecraft missions

Most spacecraft missions to comets have been flybys. In 2004, the Stardust flyby mission captured a sample of Comet Wild 2. A device shaped like a tennis racket (right) collected dust from the comet's coma and brought its cargo home.

Rosetta's 7.2 ft (2.2 m) wide steerable antenna communicated with Earth.

Rosetta

After a 10-year journey, space probe Rosetta met up with Comet Churyumov-Gerasimenko in 2014. It revealed a landscape of jagged cliffs, pits, and boulder-strewn terrain. It orbited the comet, monitoring the evolution of its coma and tails, and also released Philae to land on the 2.5-mile (4 km) wide nucleus.

Dishwasher-sized Philae bounced on to the surface and worked for two days.

- Jets of gas shoot out where the nucleus is warmed by the sun.
- Solar panels
- The rough surface of the comet nucleus is blacker than coal.

Exoplanets

We know of more than 5,000 planets orbiting other stars. Ranging from near-Earth-like to more massive than Jupiter, exoplanets follow orbits at various distances around different stars. Some orbit as part of a family, but few multiplanet systems resemble our solar system.

Far distant worlds
The known exoplanets orbit about 3,800 stars. In most cases, the star's brightness drowns the light from its planets. The planets can be detected when their gravity causes their star to wobble, or when they pass in front of the star and dim its light. Most exoplanets orbit a single star, but some orbit around a stellar pair. Saturn-sized Kepler-16b (above) orbits a small red star and a larger orange one in 229 days.

Planets around other suns
The first exoplanet found around a sun-like star was 51 Pegasi b, in October 1995. It is massive like Jupiter and hot due to its closeness to its star. It travels around the star 51 Pegasi in just four days. Exoplanets generally take the name of their star, or the name of the spacecraft or project that discovered them, followed by a letter indicating the order of discovery (starting with b).

Solar panels provide power for Kepler and its equipment.

A radiator keeps instruments inside Kepler cool.

Thrusters keep the spacecraft in position.

A high-gain antenna transmits data to Earth.

Spacecraft search
More than half the exoplanets known so far were found using the Kepler spacecraft, with many more still awaiting confirmation. In 2009–2013, Kepler studied an area of sky, monitoring 100,000 stars for Earth-like planets, and it later widened its search. Kepler used a photometer that records a star's brightness to spot slight dips in it, as exoplanets pass in front of their parent stars.

EYEWITNESS
Michel Mayor
Swiss astrophysicist Michel Mayor (b.1942) and his colleague Didier Queloz pioneered the discovery of exoplanets in the mid-1990s, thanks to their invention of an advanced spectroscope. The device split starlight into different colors to detect tiny variations caused by their motion as the exoplanets orbited the stars.

This artist's impression depicts Kepler-186f with Earth-like oceans.

Earth-like

The first exoplanets detected were similar in mass to the solar system's giant planets. Less massive ones followed—super-Earths more massive than Earth but not Earth-like in makeup, and now, Earth-like rocky planets. In 2014, Kepler-186f became the first Earth-sized planet to be found in the habitable zone of another star—today, we know of several dozen more. It orbits the star Kepler-186 every 130 days. Four other exoplanets orbit closer to the star and are too hot for water and life to exist.

Star HR 8799 is marked by an X—its light has been blocked to reveal the exoplanets.

HR 8799 b
HR 8799 c
HR 8799 d

Family of planets

About 800 stars are known to have multiple planets orbiting them. So far, our own solar system remains one of the largest, tied with Kepler-90 which also has eight planets. Three of the four exoplanets orbiting the star HR 8799 are shown above, in one of the first direct images of a planetary family captured from Earth.

Upsilon Andromedae d
Upsilon Andromedae c
Upsilon Andromedae
Upsilon Andromedae b

Orbits

Some exoplanets are so distant from their star that they take thousands of years to orbit it, while those closer may take just hours or days. Three Jupiter-type exoplanets orbit the star Upsilon Andromedae (left), but two of them—d and c—orbit at unusually steep angles.

63

Did you know?

FASCINATING FACTS

More than 2,000 years ago, Chinese astronomers recorded long-tailed comets sweeping across Earth's night sky. They called them broom stars, or hairy stars.

Comets depicted on Mawangdui silk texts (c.300 BCE) from tombs in Hunan, China

Some 19th-century astronomers thought a planet they named Vulcan existed between the sun and Mercury. Vulcan exists only in the science-fiction TV and film series *Star Trek*, as a planet orbiting a distant star.

A new mineral—armalcolite—was found on the moon in July 1969. It takes its name from the three Apollo 11 astronauts, Neil Armstrong, Buzz Aldrin, and Michael Collins.

Personal objects left by astronauts on the moon include two golf balls left behind by Apollo 14's Alan Shepard in 1971, and a family photo placed there in 1972 by Charles Duke, the Apollo 16 astronaut and 10th man to walk on the moon.

On August 5, 2013, one year after Curiosity's arrival on Mars, the rover sang "Happy Birthday" to itself. Technicians on Earth had programmed one of its soil-analysis instruments to vibrate and play the song.

More than 330 meteorites found on Earth are rocks from Mars. They were blasted off the Red Planet when asteroids crashed into it and then followed orbits that brought them to Earth.

In 2014, astronomers discovered that the asteroid Chariklo has two dense, narrow rings—the first found other than the rings around the four giant planets. Chariklo is only 155 miles (250 km) wide and orbits the sun between Saturn and Uranus.

Three toy LEGO® figures 1.5 in (3.8 cm) tall are on board the Juno spacecraft at Jupiter—the Roman god Jupiter, his wife Juno, and the astronomer Galileo Galilei.

The planet Uranus was discovered in 1781, but it may have been seen by the Greek astronomer Hipparchus in 128 BCE. He thought it was a star, as did England's Astronomer Royal, John Flamsteed, when he saw it in 1712.

If you traveled to Neptune—the most distant planet in the solar system—at 62 mph (100 km/h), it would take you 500 years to get there.

The Greek astronomer Hipparchus observing the stars

A 1991 US postage stamp showing Pluto has traveled farther than any other stamp is aboard the New Horizons spacecraft, which flew by Pluto in July 2015.

Historically, comets were seen as bad omens. When Halley's Comet passed by in 1910, Earth moved through its tail. Fearing it was poisonous, some people bought gas masks and anti-comet pills.

Images taken by the Opportunity rover after landing on Mars show what looks like a rabbit. Scientists concluded it was a piece of an airbag used to soften Opportunity's landing, or something similar.

The bunny on Mars

The Opportunity rover, working on Mars since January 2004

QUESTIONS AND ANSWERS

Who names newly discovered planets and moons?

Since the 1920s, the IAU (International Astronomical Union) has overseen the naming of space objects and their features, such as craters, mountains, and maria. Anyone can suggest a name to the IAU, but there are guidelines for each type of object. Dwarf planets, for example, are given the name of a god related to creation. Moons of Jupiter are named after the lovers and descendants of Jupiter, or his Greek equivalent, Zeus.

Who was the last astronaut on the moon?

The last mission to take astronauts to the moon was Apollo 17 in December 1972. Two of its crew, Harrison Schmitt and Eugene Cernan, made three excursions together on to the moon's surface. On the final trip, Cernan led the way out of the landing craft, making Schmitt the last man to step on to the moon. A little over seven hours later, Schmitt was the first back into the craft, making Cernan the last to step off the moon.

Harrison Schmitt collecting samples with a lunar rake

Jupiter's Great Red Spot (center), with Red Spot Jr. (below) and Baby Spot (left), June 2008

Does Jupiter have more than one red spot?

The Great Red Spot is the huge, long-running storm that rages in Jupiter's southern hemisphere. Less well known are its short-lived, smaller companions. Red Spot Jr. first appeared in early 2006 and moved across Jupiter's face below the Great Red Spot. A smaller spot—Baby Red Spot—appeared in 2008 but could not pass unscathed and was quickly consumed by the Great Red Spot.

Has Earth always spun around in 24 hours?

Earth spun about four times faster when it was younger. Friction produced by both the moon and sun's tidal effect on Earth is slowing our planet's spin and moving the Moon away. Currently the Moon moves away by about 3.8 cm (1.5 in) each year. When dinosaurs roamed, Earth's spin was about 21 hours long.

Which is the nearest exoplanet to Earth?

Proxima Centauri b orbits the closest star to the sun, Proxima Centauri, about a quarter of a million times farther from the sun than Earth. A little more massive than Earth, the exoplanet orbits its star every 11 days, within its habitable zone.

How long does it take to send a message to a spacecraft?

The farther a spacecraft travels, the longer it takes to communicate with Earth. Messages to and from rovers on Mars take 14 minutes each way. Voyager 1's signals take 21.6 hours to reach us from interstellar space.

What is the largest telescope on Earth?

The Gran Telescopio Canarias on La Palma in the Canaries, Spain, has the largest mirror, 34.1 ft (10.4 m) across. The Extremely Large Telescope being built in Chile will have a 129 ft (39.3 m) wide mirror.

Dome housing the Gran Telescopio Canarias at La Palma's observatory

RECORD BREAKERS

Longest spin
Venus has the longest spin of any planet, rotating once in 243 days. Massive Jupiter has the shortest, spinning around once in 9.9 hours. Jupiter makes 589 spins during the time it takes Venus to make one.

Slowest orbiter
The more distant a planet is from the sun, the more slowly it orbits. Neptune is the farthest and slowest of the planets. It travels along its orbit at 3.4 miles/s (5.4 km/s). Closest to the sun, Mercury is the fastest, speeding along at 29.5 miles/s (47.4 km/s).

Greatest gravitational pull
The more massive a planet, the greater its gravitational pull. Jupiter's is the greatest, at 2.4 times Earth's. If a rocket could launch from Jupiter, it would need to travel at 36.9 miles/s (59.5 km/s) to escape the planet's gravity.

Solar system facts

The eight planets form two groups. Smallest and closest to the sun are the rocky planets Mercury, Venus, Earth, Mars, and just three moons. Farther out and much colder, Jupiter, Saturn, Uranus, and Neptune have faster spins, longer orbits, and numerous moons.

SUN DATA

Diameter	865,374 miles (1,393,684 km)
Mass (Earth = 1)	333,000
Energy output	385 million billion gigawatts
Surface temperature	10,000°F (5,500°C)
Core temperature	27 million°F (15 million°C)
Average distance from Earth	92.9 million miles (149.6 million km)
Rotation period	25 days at the equator

PLANETARY DATA

	Mercury	Venus	Earth	Mars	Jupiter	Saturn	Uranus	Neptune
Diameter in miles (km)	3,032 (4,879)	7,521 (12,104)	7,926 (12,756)	4,220 (6,792)	88,846 (142,984)	74,898 (120,536)	31,763 (51,118)	30,775 (49,528)
Mass (Earth = 1)	0.06	0.82	1	0.11	317.83	95.16	14.54	17.15
Gravity (Earth = 1)	0.38	0.91	1	0.38	2.36	0.92	0.89	1.12
Rotation period in hours	1,407.6	5,832.5	23.9	24.6	9.9	10.7	17.2	16.1
Solar day (sunrise to sunrise) in hours	4,222.6	2,802	24	24.7	9.9	10.7	17.2	16.1
Average temperature	333°F (167°C)	867°F (464°C)	59°F (15°C)	-81°F (-63°C)	-162°F (-108°C)	-218°F (-139°C)	-323°F (-197°C)	-328°F (-201°C)
Closest distance to the sun in miles (km)	28.6 million (46.0 million)	66.8 million (107.5 million)	91.4 million (147.1 million)	128.4 million (206.6 million)	460.1 million (740.5 million)	840.5 million (1,352.6 million)	1,703.4 million (2,741.3 million)	2,761.7 million (4,444.5 million)
Farthest distance from the sun in miles (km)	43.4 million (69.8 million)	67.7 million (108.9 million)	94.5 million (152.1 million)	154.8 million (249.2 million)	507.4 million (816.6 million)	941.1 million (1,514.5 million)	1,866.4 million (3,003.6 million)	2,824.6 million (4,545.7 million)
Orbital period in days	87.96	224.70	365.24	686.97	4,330.59 (11.86 years)	10,746.94 (29.46 years)	30,588.74 (84.01 years)	59,799.9 (164.79 years)
Orbital speed in miles/s (km/s)	29.5 (47.4)	21.7 (35.0)	18.5 (29.8)	14.9 (24.1)	8.1 (13.1)	6.0 (9.7)	4.2 (6.8)	3.4 (5.4)
Number of moons	0	0	1	2	80	83	27	14

Spin and tilt

All planets spin on an axis (see dotted lines), tilted at an angle. Mercury is the most upright. Venus tilts so far that it spins in the opposite direction. The time taken for one spin (rotation period) is shown in the table above—Earth takes 23.9 hours per spin, but the four giant planets take less.

How far?

The vast distances between the sun and the planets are described using the astronomical unit (au). One au is based on Earth's average distance from the sun.

66

WHAT DO YOU WEIGH?

Apollo 16's John Young on the moon in 1972

Location	% of weight on Earth
Mercury	37.7
Venus	90.8
Earth	100
Moon	16.5
Mars	38.1
Jupiter	236
Saturn	92
Uranus	89
Neptune	112

If you visited other planets, or the moon, your mass (the amount of material you are made of) would stay the same. But your weight is determined by the pull of gravity on mass, and each planet has a different gravitational pull. The greater the pull, the greater your weight. To find your weight on another planet or the moon, multiply your Earth weight by the percentage shown in the table above, and divide the answer by 100.

What is a solar eclipse?

The sun is 400 times larger than the moon but 400 times more distant, so they appear the same size in our sky. When the sun, moon, and Earth are directly aligned (above), the sun is eclipsed and hidden from view. The shadow cast by the moon falls on Earth. In the darkest part, or umbra, darkness falls and a total solar eclipse is seen. Anyone in the penumbra (the rest of the shadow) sees a partial eclipse.

VIEW A TOTAL SOLAR ECLIPSE

Date	Visible from this location
04/08/24	Mexico, central US, east Canada
08/12/26	Arctic, Greenland, Iceland, Spain
08/02/27	Spain, north Africa, Saudi Arabia, Yemen
07/22/28	Australia, New Zealand
11/25/30	Botswana, South Africa, Australia
03/30/33	Eastern Russia, Alaska
03/20/34	Central and north Africa, Middle East, Pakistan, China

Key au: astronomical unit
1 au = 92.9 million miles (149.6 million km)

USEFUL WEBSITES

- For all types of NASA space missions—past, present, and future—look at **www.jpl.nasa.gov/missions**
- Follow Perseverance as it roves across Mars, on **mars.nasa.gov/mars2020** and receive its tweets on **twitter.com/NASAMars**
- Find out the latest news on NASA's search for exoplanets and life in other solar systems at **exoplanets.nasa.gov**
- Play games and learn more about space on **www.nasa.gov/kidsclub/index.html** and **www.esa.int/esaKIDSen**

PLACES TO VISIT

VISIT A SPACE CENTER
- At the Kennedy Space Center, Florida, see the rockets that launched astronauts into space, and much more.
www.kennedyspacecenter.com

VISIT A MUSEUM
- The National Space Centre, Leicester, UK, is packed with interactive galleries, a Rocket Tower, and a planetarium.
spacecentre.co.uk
- The Herschel Museum of Astronomy, Bath, UK, was William Herschel's home when he discovered Uranus in 1891.
herschelmuseum.org.uk
- The Cité de l'espace, Toulouse, France, is a theme park dedicated to space.
en.cite-espace.com/discover-the-cite-de-lespace

VISIT AN OBSERVATORY
- Palomar Observatory, California, is home to the 200-in (5 m) Hale telescope.
www.astro.caltech.edu/palomar/visitor

VISIT AN IMPACT CRATER
- Walk around the rim and peer deep inside the Barringer Meteorite Crater, Arizona.
www.barringercrater.com
- See Earth's second-largest impact crater at Wolfe Creek, Western Australia.
parks.dpaw.wa.gov.au/park/wolfe-creek-crater

Uranus
19 au

Neptune
30 au

Timeline

Earth's sky is our window on the solar system. Our earliest ancestors followed the motions of the sun, moon, and planets. Later, with telescopes, people saw the details on these objects and discovered many more. Spacecraft then became our eyes and laboratories in space, opening up these far-off worlds.

4000 BCE ▶ **500 BCE**

Nebra sky disc, Germany, c.1600 BCE

550 BCE Greek mathematician Pythagoras says the sun, moon, Earth, and planets are spherical, not flat.

4000 BCE Ancient cultures in the Near East use the sun and moon for time keeping, and think five planets—Mercury, Venus, Mars, Jupiter, and Saturn—orbit Earth.

Pythagoras

1900 ◀

1957 The first spacecraft, Sputnik 1, is put into orbit around Earth by the Soviet Union.

1930 American astronomer Clyde Tombaugh discovers a ninth planet—Pluto. Its status is changed to that of dwarf planet in 2006.

Model of Sputnik 1

1801 Ceres is the first asteroid to be found, by Italy's Giuseppe Piazzi. It is also a dwarf planet.

Yuri Gagarin, inside Vostok 1

1961 Soviet cosmonaut Yuri Gagarin becomes the first human in space, orbiting Earth in Vostok 1.

1959 The Soviet Union's Luna 2 is the first to land on the moon.

1846 German astronomer Johann Galle discovers Neptune, very close to the position predicted by French mathematician Urbain Le Verrier.

Ceres

1960 ▶ **1980** ◀

1962 American spacecraft Mariner 2 makes the first successful flyby of a planet, Venus. Mariner 4 is the first to fly by Mars, in 1965.

1971 Mariner 9 is the first craft to orbit a planet other than Earth. It orbits Mars for almost one year.

1979 The first flyby of Saturn is made by Pioneer 11.

1986 American craft Voyager 2 becomes the first and only craft to fly by Uranus. In 1989, it becomes the only spacecraft to fly by Neptune.

1973 American craft Pioneer 10 is the first to fly by Jupiter. In 1974, Mariner 10 makes the first flyby of Mercury.

1976 The first craft to land on Mars is America's Viking 1, which looks for signs of life.

Neil Armstrong on the Moon, 1969

1969 On July 21, American astronaut Neil Armstrong steps on to the moon, becoming the first human to walk on another world.

1970 The first rover to land on another world, the Soviet Union's Lunokhod 1 explores the moon for 10 months.

1975 The Soviet Union's Venera 9 transmits the first images from the surface of Venus.

Pioneer 11 image of Saturn

1200 CE

1252 The Alphonsine Tables produced by scholars for Alfonso X of Castile list the accurate positions of the sun, moon, and planets for specific dates.

964 CE Persian scholar Abd al-Rahman al-Sufi updates the astronomy of ancient Greece in his *Book of the Fixed Stars*.

Persian depiction of the Perseus constellation, from the *Book of the Fixed Stars*

1500

1424 Islamic astronomer Ulugh Beg builds his observatory at Samarkand (now in Uzbekistan).

Nicolaus Copernicus

1600

1596 The last great naked-eye astronomer, Danish Tycho Brahe completes 20 years of observations. German mathematician Johannes Kepler uses them to form his three laws of planetary motion in 1609–1619.

1543 Polish astronomer Nicolaus Copernicus suggests that the sun is at the center of the universe, orbited by Earth and the other planets.

1800

Replica of Herschel's telescope

1781 German-born English astronomer William Herschel discovers a new planet—Uranus—doubling the known extent of the solar system.

1700

1687 English scientist Isaac Newton's theory of gravity is published. It explains why the moon orbits Earth and the planets orbit the sun.

1682 English scientist Edmond Halley sees a comet, calculates its orbit, and predicts its return. Named after him, it returns every 76 years.

Halley's Comet, 1986

1655 Dutch scientist Christiaan Huygens observes Saturn and says it is encircled by a ring. In 1659, he measures the spin period of Mars.

1600

1609 The newly invented telescope is used by Italian astronomer Galileo Galilei to study the moon, planets, and stars. In 1610, he publishes his discoveries.

Galileo Galilei

1990

1992 The first Kuiper Belt object—1992 QB1—is discovered by English astronomer David Jewitt and Vietnamese American astronomer Jane Luu.

1991 Gaspra is the first asteroid encountered by a spacecraft when the American mission Galileo flies by en route to Jupiter.

2000

51 Pegasi b

1995 The first exoplanet orbiting a sun-like star is detected—51 Pegasi b.

2006 Pluto and Eris are reclassified as dwarf planets.

2012 The American rover Curiosity lands on Mars and studies whether Mars could have supported life in the past.

2014 The European Space Agency's Rosetta orbits a comet and releases Philae, the first craft to land on a comet nucleus.

2020

2021 America's Perseverance and China's Zhurong rovers land successfully and begin exploring Mars.

2016 Juno, an American spacecraft, becomes the second craft to orbit Jupiter and returns its first images from the planet.

2015 American craft New Horizons flies by Pluto before it heads to Kuiper Belt object Arrokoth.

2021 NASA's giant James Webb Space Telescope (JWST), is launched.

Juno spacecraft

69

Glossary

ANTENNA An aerial in the shape of a rod, dish, or array for receiving or sending radio signals.

ASTEROID A small rocky body orbiting the sun. Most asteroids are in the Asteroid Belt, between Mars and Jupiter.

ASTEROID BELT A region in the solar system, between the orbits of Mars and Jupiter, that contains a large number of orbiting asteroids.

ASTRONOMICAL UNIT (AU) A unit of length used in astronomy that is equal to about 92.9 million miles (149.6 million km)—Earth's average distance from the sun.

ATMOSPHERE The layer of gases held around a planet, moon, or star by its gravity.

Northern Lights (Aurora Borealis) over a lagoon in Iceland

AURORA A colorful light display above a planet's polar regions—such as Earth's Northern and Southern Lights—produced when electrically charged particles hit atoms in the planet's atmosphere and make them glow.

AXIS The imaginary line that passes through the center of a space object, such as a planet or star, and around which the object rotates, or spins.

BILLION One thousand million (1 followed by nine zeros).

COMET A small body made of snow, ice, and rock dust (called the nucleus). Comets that get deflected from their orbits in the outer solar system and travel near the sun develop a large cloud of gas and dust (the coma) and gas and dust tails.

CORE The innermost region of a planet or star.

CRATER A dish-shaped hollow on the surface of a rocky planet, moon, or asteroid. An impact crater is made by an asteroid, meteorite, or comet hitting the surface. A volcanic crater develops as a volcano ejects material.

CRUST The thin, outermost layer of a rocky or icy body, such as a planet, moon, or comet.

DWARF PLANET An almost round body that orbits the sun but does not have enough mass and gravity to clear its neighborhood of other objects.

ECLIPSE The effect observed when two space bodies are aligned so one appears directly behind the other, or one is in the shadow of the other. In a solar eclipse, when the moon passes between Earth and the sun, the sun is behind the moon in the sky. In a lunar eclipse, the moon passes behind Earth, through Earth's shadow.

EQUATOR The imaginary line drawn around the middle of a planet, moon, or star, halfway between its north and south poles, separating its northern and southern hemispheres.

EXOPLANET A planet that orbits around a star other than the sun.

FLYBY A close encounter made with a solar system object by a spacecraft that flies past without going into orbit.

GALAXY An enormous grouping of stars, gas, and dust held together by gravity. The sun is one of the stars in the Milky Way Galaxy.

GAS GIANT A large planet, such as Jupiter or Saturn, that consists mainly of hydrogen and helium, which are in gaseous form at the planet's visible surface.

GIANT PLANET Any planet that is large and massive compared with Earth. In the solar system, the four biggest planets—Jupiter, Saturn, Uranus, and Neptune—are classed as giant planets.

GRAVITY A force of attraction found throughout the universe. The greater the mass of a body, the greater its gravitational pull.

The doomed hot Jupiter WASP-12b is being eaten by its parent star

HABITABLE Suitable for living in or on. Life may exist on a planet that orbits within the habitable zone around a star.

HEMISPHERE One-half of a sphere. Earth is divided into northern and southern hemispheres by its equator.

HOT JUPITER A type of exoplanet that is more massive than Jupiter but orbits closer to its star than Mercury to the sun.

ICE GIANT A giant planet composed mainly of elements heavier than hydrogen and helium. The solar system's two ice giants are Uranus and Neptune.

INNER PLANETS The planets nearest the sun in the solar system—Mercury, Venus, Earth, and Mars.

INTERSTELLAR SPACE The region between the stars in a galaxy—in the solar system, it is the space beyond the planets.

Apollo 11's lunar module, Eagle—the first lander to put people on the moon

KUIPER BELT OBJECT (KBO) A rock-and-ice body orbiting the sun in the Kuiper Belt, beyond Neptune's orbit.

LANDER A spacecraft that lands on the surface of a planet, moon, asteroid, or comet.

LUNAR Relating to the moon, such as a lunar module built to land on the moon.

MAGNETIC FIELD The region around a magnetized body, where magnetic forces affect the motion of electrically charged particles. Earth's magnetic field, for example, is generated by flows in the planet's liquid outer core.

MANTLE A thick layer of rock between the core and the crust of a planet or moon.

MASS A measure of how much matter (material) a body is made of.

METEOR A short-lived streak of light—also called a shooting star—produced by a tiny, grain-sized piece of comet or asteroid speeding through Earth's upper atmosphere.

METEORITE A piece of rock or metal that lands on the surface of a planet or moon and survives the impact; most are pieces of asteroid.

MILKY WAY The spiral-shaped galaxy that includes the sun and about 200 billion other stars. Also the stars visible to the naked eye as a band of faint light across the night sky.

MOON A rock or rock-and-ice body that orbits a planet, dwarf planet, or asteroid.

NUCLEAR FUSION A process in which atomic nuclei join to form heavier nuclei and release huge amounts of energy such as heat and light. In the sun's core, hydrogen nuclei fuse to produce helium.

NUCLEUS (PLURAL NUCLEI) The compact central core of an atom. Also the solid, icy body of a comet.

OORT CLOUD The sphere consisting of billions of comets that surrounds the planetary part of the solar system.

ORBIT The path of a natural or artificial object around another more massive body, influenced by its gravity.

ORBITER A spacecraft that orbits a space body such as a planet, moon, or asteroid.

Incoming meteorite

OUTER PLANETS The four planets that orbit the sun beyond the Asteroid Belt – Jupiter, Saturn, Uranus, and Neptune.

PARTICLE An extremely small part of a solid, liquid, or gas.

PHASE The part of a moon or planet that is lit by the sun and visible from Earth. The moon passes through a cycle of phases every 29.5 days.

PLANE A flat, two-dimensional area. In the solar system, the planets travel around the sun at different distances but close to the same orbital plane.

PLANET A massive, nearly round body that orbits the sun and shines by reflecting the star's light.

PROBE An unmanned spacecraft built to explore objects in space—particularly their atmosphere and surface—and transmit information back to Earth.

ROCKY PLANET A planet composed mainly of rock, such as the four planets closest to the sun – Mercury, Venus, Earth, and Mars.

ROVER A vehicle driven remotely on a planet or moon.

SATELLITE An artificial object that is deliberately placed in orbit around Earth or another solar system body. Also a natural object such as a moon or any space object orbiting another, more massive body.

SHEPHERD MOON A small moon whose gravitational pull herds orbiting particles into a well-defined ring around a planet.

SOFT LANDING A controlled landing by a vehicle, including a spacecraft. A hard landing may result in the craft being destroyed, intentionally or accidentally.

SOLAR Relating to the sun.

SOLAR SYSTEM The sun and all the objects orbiting it, such as the planets and many smaller bodies.

Dying star, a glimpse of our sun's future

STAR A huge, spinning sphere of very hot, luminous gas that generates energy by nuclear fusion in its core. The sun is a star.

SUPER-EARTH A type of exoplanet with a mass greater than Earth but smaller than the ice giants Uranus and Neptune.

TELESCOPE An instrument that uses lenses or mirrors, or a combination of the two, to collect and focus light to form a magnified image of a distant object. Some telescopes collect other wavelengths besides visible light, such as radio and infrared.

21 ft (6.5 m) wide main mirror is made of 18 segments

James Webb Space Telescope (JWST)

The sunshield protects the JWST from sunlight, cooling it to less than −370°F (−223°C).

UNIVERSE Everything that exists—all space and everything in it.

VOLCANISM The eruption of molten rock on to the surface of a planet or moon through volcanic vents, often resulting in extensive flows of lava.

Index

AB
Aldrin, Buzz 14, 30
animals 26, 27
Apollo 11 spacecraft 14, 30–31
Armstrong, Neil 14, 30
Asteroid Belt 38, 39
asteroids 18, 28, 29, 33
  exploring 38–39, 43
  the moon 31
  solar system 7
astronauts 14, 23, 30–31
astronomers 9, 13, 43, 48, 50, 52, 53, 60
  see also Galilei, Galileo
atmospheres 10
  Earth 11, 22
  Jupiter 40–41
  Mars 34
  Saturn 45
  Venus 18
auroras 40
BepiColombo probe 19

CD
canyons 32, 34, 35, 55, 58
carbohydrates 16
carbon dioxide 18, 59
Carruthers, George 29
Cassini, Giovanni 46
Cassini spacecraft 50, 51
China 30, 37
Collins, Michael 30
comets 7, 40, 60–61
Copernicus, Nicolaus 12
craters 10, 18, 32, 35, 39, 58
  see also volcanoes
Curiosity ChemCam 36, 37
Darwin, Charles 27
dwarf planets 7, 8, 38, 52, 53, 58–59

EF
Earth 8, 12
  asteroids, and 39
atmosphere 11, 22
ever-changing surface 23
the moon 7
orbit, spin, and seasons 22
solar system 6
view from space 22–23
volcanoes 10
water 24–25
eclipses 17, 29, 67
Eris 7, 8
erosion 11
European ExoMars 37
exoplanets 8, 9, 62–63
extinction 27
extremophiles 27
fungi 26

GH
galaxies 9, 13
Galilean moons, 42–43
Galilei, Galileo 12, 30, 42, 44
Galileo spacecraft 50
giant planets 6, 10, 50–51
gravity 31, 40, 42
  and rings 46–47
  and tides 24
greenhouse effect 21
Halley, Edmond and Halley's Comet 60, 69
helium 40–41, 55
Herschel, Caroline 60
Herschel, William 52
Hubble Space Telescope 56, 57
human population 26
Huygens, Christiaan 44, 48
Huygens probe 49, 51
hydrogen 6, 17, 40–41, 44, 55
Hyperion (moon) 48

IJK
ice 25, 33, 35, 58
International Astronomical Union (IAU) 8
Jemison, Mae 14
Juno spacecraft 15, 42, 50, 51, 64
Jupiter 6
  atmosphere 40–41
  exploring 50, 51
  Great Red Spot 10
  mass 13
  moons 7, 42–43
Kepler, Johannes 13, 62
Kepler spacecraft 62
Kepler-186f 63
Kuiper Belt 52, 53, 58

L
Leavitt, Henrietta 13
life
  on Earth 22
  human impact on 26
  kingdoms and species 26
  search for life elsewhere 27
Luna spacecraft 14, 30, 31

M
magnetism 19, 40, 51
Mariner spacecraft 14, 19
Mars 32–37
  craters 35
  exploring 12, 14, 15, 36–37
  liquid water 11
  moons 7, 33
Mayor, Michel 62
Mercury 7, 8, 18–19
  exploring 14
  rocky surface 11, 18, 19
  view from Earth 18
Messenger spacecraft 19
meteorites 38, 39
methane 49, 55, 56, 59
microorganisms 26, 27
Milky Way Galaxy 9
monerans and protists 26
moon, Earth's 7, 28–29
  eclipses 29
  exploring 14, 30–31
gravity 24
orbit and rotation 28–29
phases 29, 30
moons
  dwarf planets 59
  Jupiter 42–43
  Mars 7, 33
  Neptune 56–57
  Saturn 48–49
  Uranus 54, 55
Morabito, Linda 43
mountains 25, 29, 30, 58

NO
NASA 14, 15, 50
Neptune 6, 9, 52, 56–57
  atmosphere 56
  exploring 50
  moons 56–57
  view from Earth 7
New Horizons probe 52, 59
nitrogen 22, 59
nuclear fusion 16
observatories 13
oceans, Earth 11, 22, 24, 25
Oort Cloud 52, 53
orbits 6, 7, 8, 28–29
  see also rotation;
  individual names of planets
oxygen 16, 22
ozone layer 22

PQR
Parker Solar Probe 17
Payne-Gaposchkin, Cecilia 17
photosynthesis 16
Piccard, Jacques 24
Pioneer spacecraft 50
planets
  defining, and naming of 8–9
  dwarf and exoplanets 8
  masses 13
  solar system 6–7
plants 26
Pluto 7, 8, 52, 53, 58–59
protists and monerans 26
Queloz, Didier 62
rings 41, 46–47, 55, 56
rivers 24, 32
robotic spacecraft
  see spacecraft
rocky planets 10–11
Rosetta spacecraft 61
rotation (spin) 29, 40, 54, 66

S
Sagan, Carl 50
sand dunes 35
satellites 17, 22, 25
Saturn 6, 44–49
  atmosphere 45
  early observations 44
  exploring 50, 51
  moons 7, 48–49
  rings 44, 46–47
Schweickart, Russell Louis 23
seasons 7, 22, 32, 56, 58
Sedna 7, 53
solar eclipse 17, 67
solar system 7, 12, 52–53
Soviet Union 14, 30–31
spacecraft
  exploring asteroids 39
  exploring comets 60, 61
  exploring Mars 27
  exploring Mercury 19
  exploring the moon 14–15
  exploring Neptune 56
  exploring the outer planets 50–51, 59
  exploring Venus 20, 21
stars 13, 62–63
  see also Sun
Stonehenge 12
storms 10, 17, 40, 41, 45, 56
sun
  ancient peoples' observations 12
  and comets 61
  energy from 16
  mass 6, 16
studying the 17, 35

T
tectonic plates 23
telescopes 12, 13, 27, 30, 57
tides 24
Titan (moon) 48–49, 51
Tombaugh, Clyde 58
Triton (moon) 57
Trujillo, Diana 37

U
United States of America 15, 27, 30–31
Uranus 6, 9, 52, 54–55
  exploring 50
  moons 54, 55
  orbit and rotation 54
  view from Earth 7

V
Venera spacecraft 15, 20
Venus 7, 9
  atmosphere 11, 20
  exploring 14
  rocky surface 21
  spacecraft 15
Vesta 38
Viking spacecraft 33
volcanoes 10, 19
  Earth 25
  Jupiter 43
  Mars 32, 34
  the moon 29, 31
  Venus 21
Voyager spacecraft 41, 43, 50–51, 54, 55, 56–57

W
water
  on Earth 11, 24–25
  on Mars 32
  on Neptune 56
  on Pluto 59
  on Uranus 55
Whipple, Fred 60
winds 17, 40, 41, 45

Acknowledgments

Dorling Kindersley would like to thank:
Ann Baggaley for proofreading, Ashok Kumar and Rakesh Kumar for DTP assistance, and Vishal Ghavri and Deepak Negi for picture research assistance.

The publisher would like to thank the following for their kind permission to reproduce their photographs:

(Key: a-above; b-below/bottom; c-centre; f-far; l-left; r-right; t-top)

123RF.com: ammit 10br; **Alamy Stock Photo:** dpa picture alliance archive 39bc, Granger Historical Picture Archive 12tr, North Wind Picture Archives 12br, DPA picture alliance 62br, Ann E Parry 23br, GL Archive 13bl, PhotoStock-Israel / Historic Illustrations 48cra, IanDagnall Computing / NASA 14bc, NASA Photo 50bc, BNA Photographic 24cb; **Dorling Kindersley:** Simon Mumford 4-5tc, NASA 43ca; **Dreamstime.com:** Andrey Andronov 69ca, Sean Beckett 27crb, Delstudio 29c, Heisenberg85 26crb, Inge Hogenbijl 65cr, Inigocia 12-13c, Igor Kovalchuk 17bc, Jamen Percy 70clb, Pixattitude 34cbl, Typhoonski 9bl, Oleg Znamenskiy 16crb; **ESA:** 19br, ATG medialab 61cb, DLR / FU Berlin (G. Neukum) 32br, 35cb, DLR / FU Berlin, CC BY-SA 3.0 IGO 33bl, J. Whatmore 11tr, NASA / JHU Applied Physics Lab / Carnegie Inst. Washington 6clb, 18-19c, R. Lockwood 33crb, NASA / The Hubble Heritage Team (STScI / AURA) / R. Sahai and J. Trauger (Jet Propulsion Laboratory) 71tr; **ESO:** Y. Beletsky / http://creativecommons.org/licenses/by/3.0 13cb, 18cl, L. Calçada and Nick Risinger / http://creativecommons.org/licenses/by/3.0 59cb (Eris), http://creativecommons.org/licenses/by/3.0 55c, 60cb, 69c, NASA / Jeff Schmaltz / http://creativecommons.org/licenses/by/3.0 39cr, M. Kornmesser, Nick Risinger (skysurvey.org) / http://creativecommons.org/licenses/by/3.0 69cb, D. Schreiner and S. Degezelle / http://creativecommons.org/licenses/by/3.0 29cr; **Getty Images:** Dea / A. Dagli Orti 60br, Archive Photos 64cra, Bettmann 58cbr, Jonathan Blair 53crb, De Agostini Picture Library 46tr, Dea Picture Library 69cr, Heritage Images / Hulton Fine Art Collection / Landesamt fr Denkmalpflege und Archologie Sachsen-Anhalt 68tc, 69tl, John Russell 52bl, Science & Society Picture Library 69cla, Gail Shumway 26tl, Stocktrek Images 30tl, Thomas J. Abercrombie 39bl, Universal Images Group 25t; Eliot Herman: 7tr; NASA and The Hubble Heritage Team (AURA/STScI): ESA / A. Simon (Goddard Space Flight Center) 10fcrb, ESA / A. Simon-Miller (NASA Goddard Space Flight Center) 65ca, ESA / Adolf Schaller 53bc, ESA / Adolph Schaller (for STScI) 59br, Erich Karkoschka (University of Arizona) 54clb, ESA / NASA / ESA / A. Simon (Goddard Space Flight Center) 6bl, 40ca, NASA / ESA / J. Nichols (University of Leicester) 40c, ESA / H. Hammel (Space Science Institute and AURA) 10crb, ESA / H. Teplitz and M. Rafelski (IPAC / Caltech) / A. Koekemoer (STScI) / R. Windhorst (Arizona State University) 13cla, ESA / M.H. Wong / J. Tollefson (UC Berkeley) 56bl, ESA / R. Beebe (New Mexico State University) 10cb, ANDREW CABALLERO-REYNOLDS / AFP 9br, Vivien Killilea / Getty Images North America 37br, Print Collector / Hulton Archive 27tc, Bettmann 17bl, Bettmann 55tr; **Getty Images / iStock:** Byelaman 2cr, 36tr; **Library of Congress, Washington, D.C.: NASA:** ESA / A. Feild (STScI) 63bc, 4l, 6clb, 11crb, 14crb, 14tr, 15l, 19tc, 19crb, 20cla, 20bl, 23bc, 24cl, 26bc, 30cb, 30-31b, 31tr, 31cr, 50cbr, 51l, 59bl (Haumea), 61cra, 64cla, 65bl, 67cla, 68cla, 68clb, 68br, GSFC / Arizona State University 30tr, Neil Armstrong 70br, JPL-Caltech / University of Arizona 5tr, 15tc, JPL-Caltech / ASI / Cornell 49tl, JPL-Caltech / Cornell / ASU 10clb, JPL-Caltech / Hap McSween (University of Tennessee), and Andrew Beck and Tim McCoy (Smithsonian Institution) 2cl, 38cr, JPL-Caltech / Keck 47cb, JPL-Caltech / KSC 42tr, JPL-Caltech / LANL / J.-L. Lacour, CEA 37cbl, JPL-Caltech / MSSS 15ca, 36-37c, 37tl, JPL-Caltech / Palomar Observatory 63clb, JPL-Caltech / Space Science Institute 45tr, 45bc, 48tr, JPL-Caltech / SSI / Hampton University 4crb, 45crb, JPL-Caltech / UCLA / MPS / DLR / IDA 38t, 68cr, JPL-Caltech / University of Arizona 33tc, 33cla, 33cra, JPL / Cornell 35cr, JPL / Cornell University 64b, JPL / DLR 42-43c, ESA 17cr, 49cl, ESA / G. Bacon 70tr, Aubrey Gemignani 19tc (MESSENGER), Goddard / Arizona State University 29cr, GRIN 50ctr, NSSDC / GSFC 40crb, Johns Hopkins University Applied Physics Laboratory / Carnegie Institution of Washington 9t, 11ca, 19ra, Johns Hopkins University Applied Physics Laboratory / Southwest Research Institute 8cl, 59cb, The Hubble Heritage Team (STScI / AURA) Acknowledgment: R.G. French (Wellesley College), J. Cuzzi (NASA / Ames), L. Dones (SwRI), and J. Lissauer (NASA / Ames) 47tc, R. Hurt (SSC-Caltech) / JPL-Caltech 53clb, JPL 4cra, 15br, 20-21c, 21cb, 25cr, 32-33cs, 35cbl, 41cl, 51ca, 55tc, 55bc, 56cl, 64c, 64-65 (Background), 66-67 (Background), 68-69 (Background), 70-71 (Background), JPL-Caltech 6crb, 28cl, 32l, 36cra, 51cfb, 62cr, 69br, Ulli Lotzmann 31tl, M. Ahmetvaleev 39t, ESA / Rosetta / NAVCAM 61b, SDO 16l, 17cl, Ames / SETI Institute / JPL-Caltech 63tr, ESA / SOHO 17cr, ESA / SOHO / SDO / GSFC 61ca, JPL / Space Science Institute 7crb, 41r, 45tc, 46ca, 47ca, 47cra, 48cr, JHUAPL / SwRI 3c, 53cb, 58bl, 58-59c, 59clb (Pluto), JPL / USGS 57tr, 4-5t, 71br, 24-25t, JPL-Caltech 8cr, 15c, JPL-Caltech 37bc, NASA / JPL-Caltech / SwRI / MSSS / Jason Major 10bl (year 2017), NOAA 6c, 22-23c, 999Wallchartcra; **Science Photo Library:** NASA / JPL / ARIZONA STATE UNIVERSITY 34-35t, Detlev Van Ravensswaay 17crb, Dr Seth Shostak 27bl, Take 27 Ltd 2bl, 10-11c; Copyright © Subaru Telescope, National Astronomical Observatory of Japan (NAOJ). All right reserved.: 43br; Dr Dominic Fortes, UCL: 57cra; Wellcome Images http://creativecommons.org/licenses/by/4.0/: Iconographic Collections 68cra; Wikipedia: 31c, CLAUS LUNAU 2c, 17c, NASA, ESA, CSA, JUPITER ERS TEAM; JUDY SCHMIDT 2tr, 41cb, PAUL D STEWART 60cl; **Shutterstock.com:** NASA / ZUMA Wire (29br), Uncredited / AP (52crb)

All other images © Dorling Kindersley